D1516656

Paul Laune

Sand in My Eyes

Sand in My Eyes

BY

Seigniora Russell Laune

ILLUSTRATED BY

Paul Laune

J. B. LIPPINCOTT COMPANY

PHILADELPHIA
AND NEW YORK

Contents

Sand in My Eyes

1 Oh, Oh, Pioneers

When I was fifteen years old my father had such a long and serious illness that the doctor advised him to leave Little Rock, Arkansas, and go to a high, dry climate.

A few years before, the land laws in the Texas Panhandle had been changed to allow nesters, or farmers, to enter the range land there and file on a section, or six hundred and forty acres. Father's brother from New York had taken advantage of this opportunity and had settled in Collingsworth County. He urged Father to visit him there, as it was certainly high and dry.

Father, who had spent his life as a teacher in Arkansas, returned from Texas enthusiastic about the wild, unsettled country. He appeared to be healthy and strong, but when he had a relapse and the doctor repeated his warning more sternly than before, Father asked Mama if she would be willing to live in the Texas Panhandle until he regained his health.

Mama, though secretly reluctant, had a strong whither-thou-goest complex and a deeply-rooted conviction that in all major family decisions, "Father knows best." She choked back her forebodings, but my older sister, Mary, sent for from New York where she had been completing her education, was frankly dismayed. Fritz, six years old, and the two-year-old Fan were too young to have opinions on the subject. I was the only one who was entirely happy.

Our home was sold. The furniture and hundreds of books were packed and shipped. A house was being built on our newly acquired land in Collingsworth County and Father went out there first, leaving the rest of us to follow a few weeks later.

After a hot, two-day trip, the brakeman bellowed the name of the station where Father was to meet us. We were hustled down the car steps beside a one-room depot squatting on a vast empty plain. Our trunks banged down from the baggage car, hand-luggage was dumped beside us, and the conductor thrust Fan into Mama's arms with a genial, "Well, well, here you are." The engine gave a derisive hoot as it scuttled down the shiny track, waving a long sooty arm of farewell.

Here we were, indeed. We huddled together in a frightened group, near some stockpens where cattle were bawling miserably. Suddenly there was a swirl of sand, a jingling of harness, and a wagon drawn by two black horses drew up beside us. A tall man, deeply tanned, wearing a broad-brimmed hat and high-laced boots, sprang from the wagon. It was Father!

We swarmed all over him. He was laughing excitedly and I realized, with a shock of surprise, that it was almost the first time

I had ever heard him laugh like that. A lean man with a pencil behind his ear strolled from the depot and helped us load the luggage into the wagon. The sun, a great red ball teetering on the edge of the world, toppled out of sight behind the horizon.

As our land was about twenty miles away, Father said we would go to the hotel for the night. The hotel, like all the other buildings in the brand-new town of Memphis, faced the wind-swept square where a brick courthouse was being built, and was a raw, unpainted, boxlike structure with a rickety little porch sticking out in front. Saddle horses and wagon teams stood quietly beside the hitching rack enclosing the square.

Mary and I walked to the hotel. Groups of men lounging against the rough-board shacks, whittling or squatting on their heels drawing in the sand, straightened and rose, and stared at us respectfully as we passed them. I thought they were admiring Mary's New York dress, in which I, too, thought she looked very elegant.

That night, the hotel swayed and leaned against the wind, and we were all, except Father, quite ill. We thought we had eaten something spoiled; but the hotelkeeper's wife said it was just the "gyp" in the water. "Gyp," we were told, was the local word for gypsum.

The next morning, weak and pale, we started out for our new home. Fritz, Fan, and I sat on a quilt spread on the floor of the wagon. (Father said a quilt was called a "soogan" in Texas.) Mary perched unsteadily on a small trunk. Mama, clutching the sides nervously, climbed to the high seat beside Father. The new wagon creaked as the horses broke into a slow trot. The wide empty land lay in an unbroken circle like a huge table-top. All around, the edge of the circle was tucked in and held neatly in place by the great hoop of blue sky. There was no road, just a trail cut through the sand. There were no trees. There was nothing to see except hundreds of grazing cattle marked with the Diamondtail brand.

At noon, Father hung nosebags on the horses and we ate a picnic lunch spread on the ground under the blazing sun. Then the journey continued. The children were fast asleep, and I was nodding when the horses suddenly started plunging and Father began yelling, "Whoa."

Leaving the trail, the horses dashed over the prairie, the wagon pitching and careening over the clumps of sagebrush. Mary was thrown from her trunk and Mama dropped to the floor and scrambled under the seat beside the little children. I crawled forward and climbed up beside Father who was pulling, tugging, and yanking on the lines.

"Pull on the brakes if you can," he panted, his feet braced against the dashboard.

The team pulled suddenly back, then plunged forward again. Something broke. The tongue slipped out of the neck yoke, the traces loosened, and the reins were snatched from Father who almost went over the dashboard after them.

The horses, now free, tore across the prairie. We sat in the wagon unharmed, and watched them flying away in the distance. We never did know what caused the trouble. It may have been heel-flies, the torment of horses and cattle on the range. It may have been some fault in the harness, for while Father was an expert horseback rider and driver of carriage teams, he had had little experience with wagon harness.

I was more excited than frightened. Life in Texas was starting out adventurously, just as I had expected. For a long moment no one spoke, then Mama asked quaveringly:

"How much farther is it?"

Father pointed. "Do you see that spot off there?" We nodded. "That's our house. It's about six miles away."

Mama started clambering to the ground. "Come, children," she commanded. "We're going to walk the rest of the way."

I begged to stay with Father and help him catch the horses, but he objected. "Go with your mother. Don't let her get too tired. Perhaps I'll catch up with you before you go too far."

We must have been a sorry-looking sight as we trudged away. None of us had ever walked more than a few city blocks in our lives. Mama was already weary from the strain of moving, the long train trip, and the wretched night in the hotel. She and Mary were hampered by trailing skirts and high-heeled shoes. Fan had to be carried. We were all afraid of snakes and of the cattle that roamed about, and between us and that far spot lay a stream that had to be crossed somehow.

Luckily for me, I was firmly planted on flat spring-heel shoes. My dress was short. I started out carrying Fan, her legs wrapped around my waist, my arms locked around her fat little body. She grew heavier and heavier. Mama took her, then Mary. We tried letting her walk, but she stumbled over the rough clumps of sod and got cactus spines and sandburs in her hands and face. Fritz kept up with us bravely, though his short little legs gave out now and then and he would sit down in a heap.

The sun blazed down like a blast from an open furnace. The wind whipped and tugged at our hats. Sandburs and beggar's-lice, those pesky weeds, clung to our skirts, bunching the cloth into odd tight folds. The cattle that we had feared gave us startled looks, threw their tails in the air, and fled. We grew so tired that fear of cattle, of snakes, of everything, left us.

When we reached Buck Creek, we found to our astonishment that it was only a trickle of water in a shallow trough of whiter, deeper sand. We stopped to rest on the low bank, emptied the sand from our shoes, and bathed our hot, swollen feet.

Just as we at last dragged ourselves up the steps of our yellow-new house, the sun, that red-faced old monster, lurched out of sight behind the horizon.

Crates and barrels covered almost every inch of space in the five rooms. A cot was in the middle of the hall, where Father had been sleeping. Mama and Mary dropped down upon it, while the little children and I tumbled down on some rolls of carpeting.

We were so weary we could scarcely move. And hungry. And worried about Father. And anxious about the wagon in which were so many of our possessions, standing alone and deserted in that wide lonely place.

A wood-burning stove was in the kitchen; but where was the

wood? And who was going to cook?

There was no laughing Louisa in the kitchen; no kind Uncle Peter in the yard to straighten out our worries; no "boy" to wait on Father, brush his clothes, shine our shoes, and run errands. Father, so learned in books, couldn't, so far as we knew, make a fire or do any other practical, down-to-earth task to save his immortal soul. Mama, who played the piano and guitar and sang beautifully, had almost never cooked a meal or swept a floor. Mary made delicious cakes and candy; while as for me, I had never done anything more useful than occasionally wash dishes and play with the babies. Yet, ignorant and ill-equipped as we were, we would have to do all the work in this new place where we had come to live.

Sitting there in that hot, cluttered, ill-planned house, isolated on the treeless prairie, our nearest neighbors two miles distant, I realized with shocking clarity that we had no business being there in the Panhandle at all. We had not the slightest acquaintance with the good earth. We knew less than nothing about farming, stock raising, or whatever people did in this bare country. We had never lived more than a block or two from a corner grocery. And we were pitifully helpless without the colored people on whom we had depended all our lives. For the first time in my sixteen years, I was afraid of the future. How were we going to manage to live? What were we going to do? Compared to us the Babes in the Woods were experienced pioneers.

I swallowed a lump in my throat as I heard again Father's excited laugh at the forlorn little depot, and remembered with what a young flourish he sprang to the ground to clasp us all in his arms. Where was he now? Walking wearily over the plains? Could he catch those wild horses?

Mama took off her gloves and flower-trimmed bonnet and pushed back her wet curls. "Well, girls," she said, her brown eyes wide with unshed tears, her lips curving in a brave, though weak, smile, "I suppose we'd better try to produce some sort of order out of this chaos. Let's see what we can find to eat." Her voice trailed off; our supplies were in the wagon, miles away.

Mary ran her fingers through her bangs and got slowly to her feet. "Sister," she said quietly to me, "you and Fritz find something with which to make a fire in the stove; I'll do the cooking."

We didn't know then about cowchips and mesquite roots, and would have been outraged at the mere mention of them. We found shavings and odds and ends left from the building of the house and barn. They burned merrily, and the already hot kitchen fairly danced with the roaring heat.

"I'm firsty," came in a wail from Fan. We were all thirsty, but had grimly refrained from mentioning it, because where would we get water? And would it be permeated with that sickening "gyp"?

Fritz found some brackish, sun-heated water in a barrel standing in a low water wagon. It was wet, at least, but it did have that unmistakable sweetish taste. We drank it; it was all we had.

Late that night, Father came in, white with weariness but driving well-behaved, docile horses. We greeted him with joy and thanksgiving, like a hero returned from the war. He had repaired the harness and we marveled at his ingenuity. Mary had supper waiting for him.

The next morning the wind had fallen to a gentle breeze. It was cool, and the prairies were covered with wild flowers that in our misery we had failed to notice the day before.

To our astonishment—Father's, no less than ours—there was a beautiful, long-legged colt beside Kate, one of the black team. Father gave him to me and I named him "Bucephalus," but Father said we had better call him "Jim" for every day and save "Bucephalus" for Sundays and holidays.

Our cousin Arthur came from Uncle Ed's place five miles away, to "help out," stayed a year, and was like a big brother. And we made a friend; Mr. Red Glenn came to finish the barn. So many nice things began to happen so quickly that my romantic dreams came to life again. Maybe we were going to be all right, after all.

Our barn rose in ridiculous elegance on the prairies where no barn had ever been before. We learned later that Mr. Glenn and others had listened to Father's plan for the barn with scandalized interest, and had strongly advised against it. But Father had been born and lived as a boy on a farm in New York where a barn was a vital necessity; *The Rural New Yorker* was his guide and mentor now that he aspired to being a farmer and stock raiser and he was determined to build a barn according to its specifications.

The people in Collingsworth County said firmly that nothing but a good windbreak was needed for range stock, and that hauling all that lumber over the sandy trail from the railroad station was pure nonsense. They also mentioned that *Farm and Fireside*, or *The Cattleman*, both Texas periodicals, were better guides than *The Rural New Yorker*. But no logic could dissuade Father from his purpose to build a barn with ample haymow and stanchions according to the blueprints he had received from New York.

Of course, there was no hay to put into the lofty mow; and we soon learned that no self-respecting horse or cow-critter could be led, driven, or dragged inside the protective stout walls of the barn, let alone submit their necks to the bars of the stanchions. They preferred to stand outside with the hot sun blistering their hides, or in the freezing wind and snow.

Mr. Glenn and Uncle Ed had also tried to discourage the building of the house, at least until we had tried living in a dugout. While many people did live in houses like ours, others were comfortable in dugouts and half-dugouts that were cool in summer, warm in winter, and almost unaffected by the ever-blowing wind. But Father, in spite of the fact that Uncle Ed had the tidiest, most comfortable half-dugout imaginable, thought he could not ask *his* family to put up with anything so crude.

So he had Mr. Glenn build a house perched on slender stilts above the hard dry ground, where in winter the icy blasts, unobstructed from Pole to Pole, whistled and howled around the thin walls and under the freezing floors. Beneath the floors the chickens, ducks, turkeys, cats, dogs and pigs found shelter from the blistering heat of summer and the rigors of winter, fighting, squealing, bumping for the choice places until we were forced to enclose the opening in order to have some peace from such carryings-on.

All year, the house complained whiningly of the wind, and the sand sifted and swirled through the doors and windows and into our eyes and hair and between our teeth. Sand rippled across the floors and ground beneath the carpets. During a sandstorm—and a sandstorm differs from the regular blowing as a tornado differs from the ordinary wind—it poured in until the floors resembled an ocean beach. Everything was covered with pure, white, clean sand. After a few months of backbreaking effort, Mama gave up, and we ripped the carpets from the floors and let nature have its way. Certainly, the floors were easier to sweep, and acquired a bone-white, scrubbed appearance from the grinding and polishing of the sharp particles. In the dugouts there was sand too, but not in such quantities as we endured. We learned to follow the example of our neighbors and turn the plates, glasses and cups upside down when setting the table for meals. We learned almost all that we ever did know about practical living from our friends on the high prairies of Texas.

Our nearest neighbors were the McDowells, who lived about two miles east of us on the way to Wellington, the county seat six miles away. They had come from South Carolina and settled "down below" in Texas until the change in the land laws permitted them to move to Collingsworth County. There were five boys: Clifford, Cecil, D'Arcy, Ezra, and the youngest, who had no name, but who had been dubbed "Yank" by his brothers because "Yankee-Doodle" was his favorite nursery song; and Yank had proved entirely adequate as a name during all his ten years. Mr. McDowell was one of the first county commissioners. They lived in a two-story house, and Mrs. McDowell's skill in managing the work for her six men seemed a miracle of efficiency to us. She was also the postmaster for the office of Clifford, named for their oldest son. I am convinced that if crowns are worn in heaven, the McDowells will wear the ones with the brightest jewels as a reward for their patient, unselfish, inspiring help to the Russell family.

About the same distance south of us lived the Bonners. They also blessed us with their friendship. They had a young son, Albert, and a married daughter, Georgia Isbell. In times of stress —and nearly all our times came under this category—either Fritz or I could be seen on a horse, galloping for help either to Mrs. McDowell or Mrs. Bonner.

Lack of water was our ever-present trial. Father had tried to have a well dug before we arrived, but after going down many feet it had been abandoned and another started. This, too, proved to be a dry hole. Like many others, we hauled water from Buck Creek or from a deep well in a neighbor's pasture some miles away. Going for water was fun, I thought, in summer. Three or four large barrels were fitted onto a low, broad-tired water wagon, and Arthur, Mary, and I would start out, singing at the top of our lungs, to return after a few hours with our precious load splashing and slopping at our backs. But when winter came, hauling water was pure torture. We nearly froze on the long cold drive and the water froze in the barrels and had to be chopped out and melted in the kitchen.

One sunny day, however, I had a disastrous experience which was entirely my own fault. *The Ladies' Home Journal* (a magazine for which Mama had a particular affection) was running a thrilling serial titled, as I remember it, "The Golden Gossip," which Mama, Mary and I were following with breathless suspense. For once, I managed somehow to get hold of the latest issue before either Mama or Mary knew it had arrived, and hastily sought a hiding place where I could read it before my elders discovered the treasure. There are almost no good hiding places on the prairies, but my anxious eyes spotted the barrels standing empty on the water wagon—and forthwith I popped into one. I had hardly reached the end of the first page before Mary and Arthur began hitching up the team preparatory to a water expedition. I went right on reading giving no hint of my presence; with luck I would finish before we reached Buck Creek.

What I did not expect was a decision to drive *across* the Creek. There was a sudden bump and lurch as the horses jumped the higher ground on the opposite side—my barrel tilted, wobbled and fell, kerplunk into the creek.

There was a hideous moment when I thought I wouldn't be able to free myself, and I had a ghastly vision of drowning under a water barrel, of all places. And then, when I did finally crawl out, wet and indignant, my sister was far more annoyed over the condition of the precious *Journal* than grateful for my safety!

We had never done a washing before going to Texas. Soiled clothes had been gathered up by Aunt Cindy, carried away and returned beautifully clean, starched, and ironed. Now we were initiated into the art of washing. Father bought the necessary equipment: a washing machine, with a lever that had to be pushed back and forth interminably to slosh and swish the water through the clothes within. Arthur put a huge black iron kettle, a regular witches' caldron, in the yard in front of the tent that housed the machine, tub, wringers, and a bench. Here Father sat and read instructions to Mama, Mary and me, from a book called, *Home Encyclopaedia, Or Things Worth Knowing, And Dedicated To Every Woman Who Aspires To Be A Good Wife And Housekeeper, And Believes That Wisdom Consists In Knowing What Is Best Worth Knowing, In The Hope And Belief That It Contains For Her Words Fitly Spoken, Which Solomon Compared To Apples Of Gold In Pictures Of Silver*. I still have that dreadful book. We followed its commands meticulously, the minute instructions for sorting linen, the manner in which the soap should be shaved and "introduced into the scalding water. . . ." It said— but I'm not going into that; washing is an old story to me now.

However, we were confronted by the peculiar phenomenon of "gyp" water. After "introducing the soap into the scalding water," it rose to the top, looked odd, and began to curdle. We did not know that that was a warning to stop, look, and listen, and dropped in the white linen. Almost instantly, a sickening sight met our gaze. Instead of the "lovely, cloud-like suds" that the book promised, in which the linen was scheduled to "billow," the linen settled down dejectedly in the bottom of the kettle, covered with a sticky, gray substance that looked, felt, and acted like putty. In spite of the book, Father, or Solomon-in-all-his-glory, there was no way of getting it off, then or ever.

We didn't know what to do, so I got on a horse and went for Mrs. McDowell. Leaving her own work and carrying a package of sal soda, she rode back home with me and showed us how to "break" gyp-water with sal soda, or lye, so that it behaves as amenably, almost, as rain water.

It was in September when Father started to plow the fields for wheat. Again, he followed *The Rural New Yorker*. He plowed deep, and then harrowed until the soil was pulverized and lay like a soft, thick, down-puff. Arthur and Uncle Ed, Mr. Mc-Dowell and his sons, all advised him to leave rough clods of sod covering the fields; when the strong winds swept the country the wheat would have a chance to send its roots down between the clods. But he thought that was a slipshod method and would have none of it.

While Arthur was with us our land was fenced and cross-fenced. We planted hundreds of cottonwood seedlings along our section lines and in a small grove near the house. These we pulled from the sand along Buck Creek. Many of them grew, as did some of the posts that took root in the sandy soil. Father, inept and unaccustomed to physical labor, entered into all this activity with enthusiasm. He seemed obsessed with the desire to convert the bare prairie into a more gracious place. Mama and Arthur tried to restrain him, but he overworked. After the bank failure in which he lost the savings of a lifetime, during the panic of 1893, he began to tire easily, and spent more and more time at his desk and on the couch.

It was then that Mrs. McDowell asked him if he would relieve her of the Clifford post office. As our family sent out and received the bulk of the Clifford mail, and as Father was in the house so much of the time, the transfer was made. Father became postmaster, and Mama, his assistant. The post office consisted of a large packing box nailed to the wall above Father's desk, divided into cubbyholes bearing the names of the dozen or so ranchers and farmers in the district.

Father thought branding cattle a cruel practice, and would have none of it. So one by one the steers from our small herd gradually disappeared on the free range.

While looking for our own strays that first winter, with the wind whipping and snarling during a furious blizzard, I found a young heifer with a newborn calf, almost frozen. I tugged and pulled and lifted until I got the tiny calf across my horse. My horse nudged and prodded the mother, whose eyes and nose were ice bound, along the trail to our barn. She was a rack of bones, too weak to resist, and was the first cow-critter to enter the stout barn walls. We called her "Bones."

Arthur helped me thaw off the snow and sleet that were caked to the cow's hide, and we rubbed her down with gunny sacks and wrapped her in blankets. We took the little calf to the kitchen, where we tried to feed it with warm milk.

It was from Bones and her calf that my herd was started. The mother bore a brand with which we were not familiar and it was two years before the rightful owner appeared. By this time, Bones' name did not fit her. She was sleek and fat and had another calf by her side. The little frozen baby that I had boosted onto my saddle was now a mother, too. So I claimed a herd of four "she-stuff," and no herd was ever more jealously guarded.

When a man rode up and inquired about the missing heifer, Father called me. I explained where and how I had found her, but pre-empting cattle in a free-range country is not lightly regarded. I got on my horse and we rode out on the range. Bones was grazing with the remnant of Father's small, unbranded herd. I pointed her out. Yes, that was the cow he was looking for. The cow was his. And naturally, the three calves kept in the small pasture near our house were also his.

I was stricken. The man's horse nosed in among the quietly grazing cattle to cut out Bones. She was gentle and would willingly come when I called her. I blinked back tears.

"If I hadn't found her and her calf that freezing day," I said,

argued a little about which one would sit on the ledge, I replied, "Oh no, here in the shade I sit."

Again she whispered, commandingly this time: "*Get down!* There's the biggest snake I ever saw, right beside you."

I lost no time in dropping from the sandy bench.

"Come on," said Mary, still in a whisper, "let's go."

"And leave it?" I asked, in horror. "Of course we can't. It might bite somebody."

We could see it plainly now. A huge circle, securely entrenched in the mass of vines and leaves. We had not heard it rattle; a horrid sound to which our ears were always attuned.

"It's asleep," Mary said, firmly. "We won't disturb it."

I knew very well it was not asleep; I could see its glittering eyes. I picked up a piece of driftwood and handed it to Mary, and armed myself with another. "You climb up on the ledge and strike down through the leaves," I ordered, "and I'll be here to catch it when it starts down."

Mary began to walk away. "I'll have nothing to do with it," she said, loftily. "That snake is asleep; we'll just go somewhere else to pick."

We could not see or hear the rest of the party. I kept my eyes on the snake. "Then," I said, "I'll strike the first blow from up there, and you be ready when it starts down." I began climbing to the bench. Then I struck through the leaves.

As I thought it would, the snake slithered down toward Mary, I right on its tail. She had no choice. She had to fight. Our brittle old sticks broke and I snatched up others. We fought and pounded but all we could do was to keep the thing from coiling in the deep sand.

It seemed to be a losing battle. Our sticks were too light and fragile. We struck frantically, almost on our knees beside the reptile. Up galloped Tom Camp, a man on the range, who knew we were picking grapes that day. He finished the task.

Mary and I were ready to collapse. "How did you know to come?" I gasped.

"How did I know?" he repeated, laughing. "You girls were

screaming as though Indians were scalping you. They could have heard you in Wellington."

Tom, who was six feet two inches tall, picked the snake up by the tail and held it level with his head. The big flat head lay along the ground. There were twenty-three rattles, which we took home to put in Mama's guitar. We had been told that rattles improved the tone but Mama rebelled and emptied them all out. She said she didn't care for the improvement.

Every spring, gardens were planted with abiding faith and tenderly cared for until the hot wind and sand, and the absence of rain, caused them to wither and die. But melons! Every kind and description flourished in the sandy soil. Pickles and preserves were made from the rinds—those that were not used to make water troughs for the chickens and pigs.

Peanuts did well, too. Uncle Ed was an expert peanut grower and shipped them in commercial quantities. The fragrance of roasting peanuts poured from every kitchen. There was always a huge pan in the oven, and another ready for eating. Candy-making with peanuts and the syrup made from specially-grown cane and sorghum became an art in which every girl excelled. Mary, with her talent for cooking, was successful in concocting several varieties of candy from these lowly ingredients. Though our life was so different from any we had known before, we felt no lack and had fun in contriving new ways to meet old needs.

The wheat that Father had planted in the fall, in the deep-plowed, smoothly-harrowed fields, came up beautifully and was a carpet of beautiful green. And then—the winds came. Every spear was swept from the fields, taking the loose soil with them. The fields were left as bare as though no plow or harrow had ever turned the sod.

Father stood at the window watching the cloud of sand and wheat. All that toil. All his bright hopes for a full crop, an abundant yield. Gone, all gone in a matter of minutes.

2 Texas Society and Schoolteaching

When we first went to Texas I had been considered too young to go out with young men, but at seventeen I entered Society.

Mary and I had been surprised and a little disappointed to find that cowboys bore little resemblance to our ideas of what they should look like. When they came to see us, their dress was very little different from that of the young men we had always known. Their hats had wider brims, but that was to protect them from the sun. They wore boots with run-under heels, which were practical for riding horseback. A good deal of attention was given to bright scarves and flannel shirts, but chaps were never worn except for protection from the cold, or for riding through mesquite or other brush, and patent-leather pumps were carried to dances in saddlebags.

In Wellington, there was a general store, a school, a saloon, at which we girls did not even look, a hotel and blacksmith shop. There were also a few dwellings where we were welcomed with satisfying, flattering cordiality. We found the friends we made in our new home much like people whom we had always known. There was less formal education among them, but they were well educated in generosity, innate courtesy, and practical living. Young men from Eastern colleges, Harvard, Princeton, and Yale, and one or two writers, came to the country during the roundups for work, adventure, or local color.

The courthouse, standing in the center of the square in Wellington, with its large District courtroom, became a place for social gatherings, public meetings and young people's parties. We could see the lights from our place six miles away. There were no church buildings but when a minister was sent by the governing body of one denomination or another, services were held in schoolhouses or some other convenient place, sometimes in homes. Whole families would come in wagons from all over the country and camp near by, so as to be ready for the morning service. Young people rode their ponies, and everyone brought well-filled baskets of food. After the morning service, dinner was spread on tablecloths over blankets on the ground, and the entire congregation sat around like one large family. When no one could eat anything more, the dogs lying beneath the wagons were called and fed. The men withdrew in groups to discuss crops, cattle and the weather, while the women sat together to nurse their babies, visit, and some to "dip snuff."

I watched this snuff-dipping with fascination. I could not take my eyes from the little sticks with their chewed, fuzzy ends. They were stirred round and round in a small can until a mass of brown powder clung to them. This was then taken deftly into the mouth where it was wabbled around. Mama tried to divert my attention: "Nonie, wet this cloth and wipe Fan's face and hands." "Nonie, come and . . ." but I would always return to hear the gossip about the kind of wood that made the best "breshes." One woman had a bresh that she got in Alabama and had used for years.

After an hour of resting and visiting, which was as inspirational and as soul-saving as the preaching to these people who had so few social contacts, an afternoon service of preaching and hymn-singing was enjoyed. Then the last of the food was eaten, the children were packed in the wagons, the horses were mounted, and we rode back over the sandy roads to our isolated homes.

Everyone belonged to a church "back home" and remained loyal to its precepts, though there was one thought that seemed to be common to all denominations, whether Methodist, Campbellite, Baptist, or Presbyterian. They were all opposed to dancing, and if a fiddle, mouth organ, jew's-harp or any instrument that made music was employed as an accompaniment for our entertainment, that was dancing, and was wicked. But if we sang while we "played" such games as Virginia Reel, Weavly Wheat, Old Dan Tucker, Skip-to-my-Lou, Needle's Eye, Come-In-and-Out-the-Window, and countless others, that was all right. Square-dancing, too, was not frowned upon if we sang the words the caller shouted. These words and tunes were often improvised on the spot, and caused as much merriment as the "playing."

We were Methodists and Episcopalians. Father could not understand why, when the young people were at our house, Mama did not play the piano or guitar for us to dance to. I don't think he ever did understand the fine distinction between "dancing" and "playing."

It was strange and a little sad to watch Mary at these "play-parties." Dressed in the Worth gowns our aunt had had made for her and brought from Paris, she stood small and ladylike, her brown eyes anxious and bewildered, her hands outstretched to whomever would take them. She was pushed here and there by the other dancers, in the midst of the choking dust and the non-sensical singing, but she never really learned to be a part of the group.

Rows of older people lined the walls at these parties. We never felt that they were restricting our fun, or that they were chaper-ones guarding our morals. They gave us a sense of togetherness, sometimes participating and introducing steps that we did not know, and adding to our enjoyment by laughing and clapping, and calling encouragement to the ones on the floor. At best, there were so few of us that the more who came to share in the fun, the merrier for all.

Wherever we went we had to ride horseback. We learned to wear coats even in the hottest summertime to protect us from the blistering sun. Before we knew this, Mary and I wore our white dresses with lace and embroidered yokes with the result that designs of flowers and leaves were almost permanently ta-tooed across our shoulders.

I envied Lena Alexander, a pretty pink-and-white blonde, her ability to bleach the freckles that came out on her fair skin after an afternoon in the sun. Mary, being dark, did not freckle at all. The freckles that I acquired yielded to no such simple treatment, but as I considered a snow-white complexion positively essential to a young lady in Society, I had to resort to bathing my face in buttermilk, which dried and crackled most uncomfortably. Mama suggested that I wear a mask made from one of Fan's small pillowcases, with holes cut out for my eyes, and long stock-ings pulled over my hands and arms. Such unsightly covering could not be worn before people, but it was a blessing when racing over the prairies alone, hunting stray cattle or going on errands. If I saw anyone approaching, the mask and stockings were quickly removed.

As we left Little Rock before I graduated from high school, Father had mapped out a pretty rigid schedule of study for me, which I followed in a haphazard way. It was not that I disliked studying, but there were too many interesting things to do and see, too many places I wanted to investigate on my small black pony which I rode sidesaddle, as all women did in those days. It would have been the deepest disgrace to ride astride. Mr. Hamilton, who owned the store in Wellington, got me a saddle that was the pride of my heart—a deep-cushioned, Gallop and Frazier saddle with leap-horn and bucking strap, covered with cream-colored leather as soft as velvet. A cream-colored bridle and martingale with elaborate cabachon accompanied the saddle, but this elegance usually hung in the barn while I used a service-able dark leather bridle, with no martingale.

There was no school in our district, though there were a number of children of school age. One day, when he was waiting for the mail, Mr. Tom Goodnight, whose daughter and son were ready for school, suggested that Miss Nonie would make a fine teacher.

My Father looked startled. I did teach Fritz for an hour or two each day, but Father certainly had no faith in my ability to take on a school.

At seventeen, I did not share his skepticism. Of course I could teach. All my life had been spent among teachers. Father had organized the State Teachers' Association of Arkansas and was even then its honorary president. He had had a class of teachers who met every week in his study to whom he taught Pedagogy, but even though I reminded Father that I had often listened to his lectures, he was unimpressed.

But Mr. Goodnight must have spoken to others, for Mr. Clement, Mr. MacIntosh, Mr. McDowell, Mr. Jones, and others appealed to Father to let me start a school. There seemed to be no very good argument against it. I wanted to; and Father admitted that Fritz was learning.

"You understand that you are not old enough to apply for a certificate to teach, and you cannot receive any pay?"

Yes, I understood that, but I wanted something grown-up to do. So Father finally said to Mr. Goodnight, "I don't think

Nonie is in any way qualified to teach, but perhaps it won't harm the children to come here and try to learn."

So the children came to "my school" until a real one was opened in the district, with a real teacher, with a real certificate. After that, I returned to my own desultory studying for a while.

The cloud that darkened my private little world, was the fast-approaching time when Mary would marry Harry Dodge, a newspaperman, and return with him to Little Rock. We had been together so constantly since coming to Texas that the four years' difference in our ages meant nothing any more. I could not imagine that there would be any fun in life without her.

A few days before Mary and Harry were married, she and I were at a party in Wellington. Tank Swafford, our sheriff, arrived late and sat down wearily beside Pa Cocke, who was county treasurer.

"I just got back from the Dozier district across the river," he said. "They need a teacher there, the very worst way. There's a good little schoolhouse. I talked to George Caperton and John Howe, and they asked me to see about finding someone."

I had just been moaning to Mr. Cocke about how lonely I would be after Mary's marriage.

"Why couldn't I apply for that school, Mr. Swafford?" I asked, breathlessly.

Mr. Swafford was a large, kindly man with a gentle voice and merry eyes.

"You have to have a certificate to teach in the public schools, sister."

"Yes, I know; I'll get one," I replied.

"You have to be eighteen years old, kid." He patted my shoulder.

"I'm eighteen, honest. Tell me the names of the people, Mr. Swafford, and how to go see them."

I could hardly wait to get home and tell Father and Mama. They were no more encouraging than Mr. Swafford had been. Father was one of the examining board and remembered that it did not meet for another month.

"You'll have a month in which to prepare for the examination," he said, "and it will be much better for you to wait until you have a certificate to present to the school board before you apply for the school."

But I couldn't wait. Mary was leaving and I would be alone. So at dawn the day after the wedding, I saddled Jim and started out to ask for the Dozier school.

It was well past midnight when I returned home, hungry and jubilant, and announced that I had been promised the school. I would begin next Monday. I had promised to teach nearly a month without a certificate, until I could take the examination. Of course, if I did not pass, I could not receive any pay, and would be out my board bill. I had arranged to board with a family who lived in a comfortable dugout, about a mile from the school.

The day of the examination, Father was ill and could not serve on the board. I went into Wellington, and learned that the papers were to be sent to Austin for grading. Having expected that Judge Small, who was also county superintendent of schools, would do this, I had some bad moments. However, in due course I was notified that I had passed, and a certificate, second grade, was granted me. Father was pleasantly astonished, and so was I.

My school was a one-room frame structure, perched brashly on a slight rise, about a mile or so from the George Caperton land. There was a barrel of water with a tin dipper in one corner of the room. The water and the wood for the airtight stove were hauled to the school by parents. Wooden benches served for seats. Father let me have a blackboard he had used in "institute work" in Arkansas, made in the manner of a roller-towel, which was a great help.

As all but four of the thirteen pupils were of two Caperton families, with Evelyn, of the George Capterton brood, the oldest, it seemed the most natural thing in the world for her to take charge of such discipline as there was.

"Willie," she would say, "stop pulling Georgie's hair."

"Albert, take your feet off of Nanny Howe's apron."

"Margie, stop making that noise with your slate-pencil."

"Jim, stop pushing Willie Howe."

"Clair, sit up; don't hunch your shoulders that way."

It never occurred to me, and I am sure it did not to the children, that this was not the usual way for a school to be governed. There was little, if any, pupil-teacher distinction. We were really a group of children working together. Discipline, as such, was unknown. We all played Ring-Around-a-Rosy, Town-Ball, and Pull-Away, at recess, and studied hard during the school hours.

And I received a salary. Twenty-seven dollars a month, as I remember. Riches beyond imagination!

Life in the Dozier district brought me to an entirely new circle of friends. Though I was two or three years older than Evelyn Caperton, we became contemporaries in social affairs. She had two older brothers, who were at work away from home, and a married sister about my age. Having never had an older brother, I believed hers gave her an advantage in worldly wisdom that I lacked. I asked her advice and relied on her judgment in matters that demanded wise decisions. Evelyn was a beautiful girl, possessed of a dignity of character unusual in one so young. She shared with her mother the responsibility of seven younger brothers and sisters.

The land on which the Capertons had settled near Dozier Creek was nearly fifty miles from the railroad station. It was imperative to provide a home in the shortest possible time, but to haul lumber from the railroad through the sandy trail was out of the question, even with the aid of the powerful strength of Jim and John, the finest span of Alabama mules in that part of Texas, so a half-dugout was the temporary solution.

As the Capertons, like our family in the Clifford district, were the heaviest contributors to the United States mail service, Mrs. Caperton was appointed as postmaster of the Dozier post office. To the Caperton dugout the people came, ostensibly, to get their mail. On Sundays, especially, the yard around the dugout was

3 Romance

While I was teaching across Salt Fork a young man, Fred Mason, boarded with my parents and taught the Clifford school. I seldom saw him, for when I went home over the weekends he went to Hedley, a flag station on the Rowe Ranch, about twenty miles northeast, to see Elaine Proctor, the girl he was engaged to marry. She was a fragile, white-and-gold blonde, with a gentle gaiety. We called her, "Elaine the fair, Elaine the lovable, Elaine, the lily maid of Astolat."

The Rowe Ranch was started by Alfred Rowe, who was later joined by his brothers, Vincent and Bernard. The men, being Britishers, were considered eccentric and unpredictable by the Texans whom they employed and with whom they were never very chummy or intimate. But the Rowes had a talent for selecting men of great ability and unquestioned integrity to act as manager and range boss, while they commuted back and forth across the Atlantic. In its heydey, the ranch was spread over parts of four counties.

Our social lives were confined to three ranches, the RO where Elaine lived, the Rockingchair where Evelyn lived, and the Diamondtail where I lived.

The Rockingchair, like the RO, was British-owned, but James Charles Hamilton Gordon, Earl of Aberdeen, and Edward Marjoribanks, Baron Tweedmouth, were less successful ranchers than Alfred Rowe who did spend a good deal of time in Texas in spite of his frequent trips back to England. It had been the hope of the titled owners to colonize a Little England in the Texas Panhandle, with lordly estates and manor houses where guests would be entertained by wolf and rabbit hunts complete with blooded hounds and horses imported from Britain. Greyhounds and staghounds were indeed brought over and their less aristocratic descendants still run over the prairies of Collingsworth County, but the dream of vast prosperity and a sanctuary for "younger sons," as well as for well-born remittance men who for various reasons were no longer welcome at home, died a lingering death. Like a good many other ranches established as a result of stories circulated in England about the fabulous profits to be picked up with little effort in the American West, the Rockingchair suffered from what might be called absentee-mismanagement.

The Diamondtail, on the contrary, had been started by two canny cowmen, the Curtis brothers, of whom Old Bill was the most famous. Fantastic stories were told us by the men on the range, of his honesty, his courage and daring, his energy and shrewdness. His rule of conduct was simple: "What's mine, I aim to keep; what's the other fellow's, is none of my business."

Thanks to the hospitality of these three ranches, not all our entertainment was as simple as the parties in the Caperton dugout, but it was meager enough to make us envy the gay life in Woodward, Oklahoma Territory, as reported by the men from our range who trailed cattle there for shipment to Eastern markets.

Woodward, a newly formed town in the Cherokee Strip, was a division point on the Santa Fe Railroad, and was becoming one of the important cattle-shipping stations in the Southwest. As soon as Fred Mason closed the school term at Clifford, he told my parents and Elaine goodbye, and hurried off to Woodward to see if its reputation for get-up-and-get was based on more than rumor.

In the glowing letters he sent back were frequent references to a young lawyer, Sidney Benton Laune, a friend he had made in Woodward. He wrote Elaine, "Ask Miss Nonie to visit you when I come this summer to see you. I think I can induce Sidney Laune to come with me; and I want him to meet her. I've told him about her and Professor and Mrs. Russell. I'm sure they will like him." We suspected that Mr. Laune's having a team and buggy with which to make the trip to Texas may have had a good deal to do with Frank's exaggerated accounts of my parents' and my charms and his eagerness to have him meet us. . . .

I had just closed the term of school in the Dozier district and was soon to begin a term in the Happy Valley district, when Elaine's invitation came. She and her friends had planned a picnic for the entertainment of her guests following the day of the young men's arrival and I went up on the train a day or two before they were expected.

As we prepared the fried chicken, deviled eggs, beaten biscuits, potato salad, pickles and cakes for the picnic dinner, we kept running to the window to look out over the prairie.

Like Bluebeard's frantic wife, Elaine would call to me as I peered through the field glasses: "Sister Anne, Sister Anne, do you see anybody coming?"

And I would reply: "Not yet; not yet. Nothing but the green grass growing, and the hot wind blowing."

The day they were to arrive passed, and the next morning we heard that heavy rains had fallen east of us and had made torrents of the rivers and creeks. There was no way for the men to let us know that they were pushing on as fast as they could, or for us to let the other picnickers know they had not come. Or for us to keep the food we had prepared from spoiling.

So Elaine and I, with our well-filled baskets, were seated in her buggy ready to start to the picnic without them when the young men drove up, their horses and buggy covered with mud though, as they had stopped at a near-by ranch to wash up and change their clothes, they themselves were spick and span.

When they sprang from the buggy and came forward to greet us, I was conscious that the stranger who was to be my escort during his stay was not in the least like the picture I had drawn of him in my mind, though until that moment I was not aware I had visualized him at all. He was older than I had expected, more mature and serious, with an air of complete self-assurance. He was about Fred's height, six feet. While Fred laughed aloud and shouted boyishly, Mr. Laune smiled readily and easily, showing unexpected dimples high on his cheekbones beneath his eyes and above the tucked-in corners of his mouth.

He looked at me steadily, trying to see behind the thick brown Merino veil tied around my face, hat, and beneath my chin. I grew self-conscious and heard myself ask:

"Where are you from?"

He chuckled; his voice was low and quiet. "Nebraska, Colorado, Oklahoma, in that order. I might mention a few years in Ohio and Michigan."

Elaine's parents and young brother and sister came out to welcome Fred and his friend. As soon as the introductions were over, Fred suggested that I ride with Mr. Laune to the picnic and he would go with Elaine in her buggy.

The exchange was made, but as the others drove happily away, Mr. Laune dragged a suitcase from the back of the buggy and took from it a long linen duster that he put on and buttoned from neck to toes. So covered he began to unhitch the horses from the buggy, explaining that he would curry the horses and clean the buggy before we started. I watched impatiently as Elaine spun away down the pasture road to the big gate.

He led the horses to the water tank where he washed and dried and brushed them until they shone like satin. He cleaned the mud from the buggy wheels and from the harness, and assured me that when we returned that evening he would do a more thorough job. I sat perched alone in the buggy while he entertained Elaine's father and brother with incidents of the trip. At last, with everything to his satisfaction, he hitched the team to the buggy, removed the duster, and cheerily took his seat beside me, where I sat simmering in brown veiling and displeasure.

If he noticed my haughty silence, he gave no sign, and seemed utterly unconscious of having slighted me in any way at all. In fact, I began to realize that he had complimented me by making the buggy in which I was to ride neat and tidy. I felt ashamed of having been so petty.

It had been a long time since I had talked to anyone from the outside world. He made the ride gay with incidents of his college days in Ohio and Michigan. He told me the wonders he had seen two years before at the World's Fair, in Chicago, after having just been graduated from Ann Arbor. And he told me of the spectacular Run which opened the Cherokee Outlet to settlers, and in which he had participated. Moreover, I think nothing of the drama of that amazing bit of history was lost in the telling. . . .

We discovered that we both loved music, and had the same taste in poetry. He confessed that he had had little time for reading fiction, other than that required in school and college.

"Now," he remarked, "we have a good start toward a lasting friendship!" Then, turning to me, he said casually, "I can't tell whether it's your funny, inconsistent manner of thinking, or your voice, that I love you for most."

I stared at him through my veil. Before I could think of a reply, he went on:

"I like your voice better, I think, than any girl's I ever heard. I imagine you have a pretty mouth and eyes, but of course I haven't seen them. You are," he turned to look at me critically,

"just the right size." Then, with a quick grin, "There; that was done very well, don't you think? You see, I'm not very well versed in such matters, but Fred told me that all Southern girls expect to hear—we-ell, things like I've been saying. Did I do it all right?"

"You did it perfectly," I replied, stiffly. "With your subtle manner, you should go far—with Southern girls."

He leaned back with a low chuckle. "Now, tell me about yourself. Where are *you* from? And how did you get here? What do you do when you're not visiting Miss Elaine so I could meet you, and when you're not riding with me?"

Fortunately, I felt, we arrived at the picnic grounds before I caught my breath sufficiently to answer—or decide not to answer —the questions of this brash young man.

The wind-swept spot, bare and smooth where cattle had bedded, was in a cluster of cattle-rubbed cottonwood trees near a creek that was usually a sandy, dry draw. It bore no relationship whatever to pictures of beautiful recreation parks, grassy and tree-shaded. But we were not critical. This little bit of shade near a stream seemed ideal to us.

A crowd of Elaine's friends were already there. I knew some of the girls and many of the young men. Elaine and I joined the group while Mr. Laune and Fred attended to hobbling out the horses. When this was done, they came strolling back to us.

We had removed our thick veils and I saw Mr. Laune give the girls a puzzled glance. We were all dressed in white, and all wore large, flower-trimmed hats. I realized that Mr. Laune was searching out the girl he had brought. I knew my voice would betray me so when the introductions were made I smiled and did not speak.

After a moment, he settled down on a log beside me. "Pretty bracelet you have on," he remarked. "I noticed it as we drove along."

The next evening, he asked me to marry him.

I was sitting on the counter in the tack room watching him oil and polish the harness. He proposed with the same politeness with which, a few moments earlier, he had asked: "Will you hand me the soap, please."

I was surprised, but not too overwhelmed. I assumed, after the first moment of astonishment, that he was practicing the technique Fred had advised for "Southern girls."

Elaine and Fred were near by and I entered into what I thought was a silly joke by calling them to witness. To my embarrassment, Mr. Laune was not amused. His lips tightened when we laughed, and he looked offended. He said, with narrowed eyes, that perhaps he had been "a little precipitous," but that he had "such a short time in which to prepare my brief and plead my case" he "could not take the usual roundabout method of courtship."

This dignified speech mortified me dreadfully, and I mumbled an apology. "We scarcely know each other," I explained reasonably. "And I thought you were just following Fred's advice."

"No, not that," he replied patiently. "I thought we could get the most important matter settled and go on from there to get better acquainted. I thought it would save a lot of time."

"But, but—we don't even—love each other," I persisted.

"Don't we?" he asked quietly, his gray eyes fixed steadily on mine until I felt the heat creeping up and beating in my cheeks. "As you say, we've known each other a very short time, and perhaps you're not aware of the fact, but I believe we do."

"But I—there's a man—"

"Yes?" judiciously. "Then I suggest you notify him at once that there has been a change in your plans. There's a little matter in Oklahoma—not too complicated, you understand—but a slight involvement that should be adjusted, also."

With Fred and Elaine standing there grinning like Cheshire cats, it all sounded pretty silly, and a little frightening, too.

The next day the four of us drove to Clifford, after which the two men would return to Oklahoma. As usual, Fred and Elaine were together, and I with Mr. Laune. Along the way, the matter that seemed uppermost in his mind was further discussed.

"Why do you think it would be—nice—to live with me?" I asked.

He considered this for a while. "I think you would be nice to live with," he quoted me, "because you seem to be so happy. You sing and laugh and get so much pleasure from such simple things. Everything seems like fun to you. Isn't that," he looked at me anxiously, "a pretty good reason for thinking you would be 'nice' to live with?"

"Oh, but I'm not like that at all! I just have to be happy with simple things, because they are all we have here."

"Exactly," he nodded, "that's what I said."

After meeting my parents, Mr. Laune and my father sat on a bench beside the house in the yard. During their conversation, I learned later, the subject of my marrying him was reasonably and thoroughly discussed. Even the "slight involvement in Oklahoma" was explained.

He told of his plans and ambitions for the future, in which he calmly included me. He made no formal request, but took Father into his confidence. Father was, I think, wholly at a loss. He was perplexed and confused by this unusual approach to his daughter's future. After he had made his intentions clear, and had not been rebuffed, Mr. Laune turned his attention to having a good time. He made himself useful wherever he could, assisting in every indoor and outdoor task, as he had done in Elaine's home.

Both he and Fred had pleasing voices and loved to sing. The piano and guitar were never quiet while we were in the house. "The Bullfrog on the Bank," "Sweet Marie," "A Bicycle Built for Two," and "After the Ball," were all shouted to the rafters. They taught us a parody on "After the Ball":

> After the Strip was opened,
> After the Run was made,
> After my horse was buried,
> After my debts are paid,
> Then I shall be contented,
> For many have lost their grip,
> Many a man has wished he'd been hung,
> Ere going to The Strip.

The morning they started back to Woodward, Oklahoma Territory, Mr. Laune assured me that he would return the following summer and we would be married. He spoke very clearly, so that Fred, Elaine, and my parents, all standing beside his buggy, could hear.

During the months that followed, his letters brought fascinating accounts of events in Woodward. The townsite fight, in which Dean and Laune represented the "East Woodward faction," was progressing nicely in their favor. Temple Houston, the son of General Sam Houston, the idol of Texas, killed a fellow-lawyer, Ed Jennings, brother of Al Jennings, who later became a train robber, during a court trial in which the two were on opposing sides of a case. In the opinion of many, the three Jennings brothers and their father, a judge, were trying to run things in the courts. However that may have been, Houston was acquitted of murder in the trial that followed. There were also stories of house parties at Fort Supply, plays by the Dramatic Club, and other club meetings of the young people. In his letters he often referred to "next summer, when we will be married."

I showed Evelyn Caperton one of his letters and after reading it she said:

"Nonie, I believe you'll be sorry if you don't marry him."

I began to think perhaps Evelyn was right.

The school I was teaching would close in July, so I wrote to tell Mr. Laune I would be ready to marry him if he came at that time.

A letter came from Elaine asking me to come to see her as soon as possible. I thought, and hoped, she was planning to marry Fred when he came with Mr. Laune for our marriage. After closing my school and spending a few days at home, I went to the station on the mail hack with Charlie Jones, the mail carrier, and took the train. When it squealed to a stop at the Rowe flag-station long enough for me to be tossed to the prairie, I found Elaine waiting for me.

She looked ill. After we had settled ourselves in the buggy, before starting the drive to her home, she handed me a letter from Fred to read.

It began: "My Beloved," and was the most incomprehensible letter I have ever read. He told her how much he loved her, and that he could never write her again. He told her how wonderful she was, and what an inspiration she had always been to him, and how the sound of her voice and her soft laughter rang in his heart. He said he prayed for her forgiveness; and hoped that she might find happiness without him, for he had married another girl, and had left Woodward.

I read and re-read the letter in stunned silence. We could not, nor did we ever, understand.

It was during this week with Elaine, when she went about white and strained-looking but with no other indication of heartbreak, that I met a young man from the South. He was a graduate of a Southern college, clever and witty and well versed in the extravagant phrases that Fred had advised Mr. Laune to cultivate.

I knew from the start this might lead to a situation that would call for decisive action. But we girls had fallen in and out of love many times, with no painful after-effects on either side, and this was such a fascinating experience that I let it drift, telling myself that it would end as such things always ended, with comfortable indifference on both sides.

I did not tell him about Mr. Laune. I played the game lightly, but with an inward excitement and the hope that this was Romance, and would last.

I did not mention to Elaine that I was involved, or thought I was, in a love that was serious. She was having difficulty enough. She told her family and friends that her engagement to Fred had been a mistake and was now terminated. I think they were all glad. "Fred," her father said, "was all right, but a perennial boy."

I wrote to Mr. Laune, asking him to release me from my promise, but two things happened before my letter could be mailed.

Father forwarded a long letter from Mr. Laune, written nearly two weeks before from his home in Nebraska, where he had been called by the death of his father.

"Father was stricken suddenly," he wrote, "and while we were all together, Mother, my sister and two brothers asked me if I would come back here and take care of Father's law, loan, and real estate business until his estate can be settled. It will take about three years. I hope you will not mind being rushed into this change but it seemed the only thing I could do. I am leaving for Woodward tomorrow, and as soon as I can arrange matters will start at once for Clifford, where we will be married. Then, after one day in Woodward, we shall leave for Nebraska. I shall not terminate my partnership with Judge Dean as I shall want to return there and resume my practice."

A note from his mother was enclosed with his letter, telling me how glad she was, especially at this time, for the interest a new daughter would bring. She hoped I would be willing to marry her son right away, and that I would not mind living in the old home with her until better arrangements could be made.

While I was reading this, there was a swish of buggy wheels, and the man who had filled my thoughts for a week, rushed into the room. Before I could get my mind in working order he began to pour out a flood of plans. "Come on; this minute. Let's go to town and get married right away. Then we'll drive to Clifford and surprise your parents" (it would certainly have surprised them!) "and keep right on going."

All the gay banter, joking, and make-believe love was gone; there was such sincerity and earnestness in his voice that my heart lifted in happiness. I wanted to do as he said. But I was holding in my hand a letter from the man I had already promised to marry.

Turning to him, I instinctively held out the letter, confident that he would understand and together we would find a way out of this dilemma. Absurdly, the thought flashed into my mind that Mr. Laune would know just how to help me.

He read it in stunned silence, his eyes growing cold with anger. Then he asked between set teeth, "Why haven't you told me about this before?"

"Because," I stammered, "you hadn't told me, really, that you love me. I was—I was—afraid you might say—you might think—"

He interrupted, "Why, you knew I loved you. I've told you in every language I know."

"I know, you—joked—about it," I replied miserably, "but I—I—"

"You're a darned little hypocrite." He laughed contemptuously. "I'd have staked my life on your honesty, and all the time—"

He walked out of the house, and drove away.

I thought I was dying. I wanted to call him back and pour out a torrent of explanations and apologies. But he had called me a hypocrite. He had shamed me to the depths of my soul.

The only thing I had to sustain me, and it was scant comfort, was that I had always met the lightness of his manner with equal lightness, parrying and brushing aside any show of deep sentiment. I kept hugging this pride-saving shred of comfort to myself.

I told Elaine and her parents that I must leave for home at once, and showed them Mr. Laune's letter. He might be even then on his way to Clifford.

When I reached home I went to bed with a chill. I was sure that I would waste away from a broken heart. But Mama said it was a summer cold. "Nothing makes one feel as miserable as a summer cold, honey," she said.

The next day Mr. Laune arrived, and I got out of bed, the unhappiest creature alive. I thought I could not face him.

The instant I saw him, I felt such a sudden surge of gladness that I flew into his outstretched arms and began to cry. I am sure that he and my parents were no more astonished at the warmth of my greeting than I was.

We walked out to the cottonwood grove near the house and there, without interruption, he listened patiently while I told him the whole humiliating story. When I finished I asked fearfully, "Do you think I'm dishonest? That I'm unreliable and fickle?"

"I think"—he smiled—"that you needed something that would

make you sure of how you feel. Are you sure that you are sure, now?"

I nodded. I was sure that I was sure.

4 Honeymoon

It was the twentieth of July, 1896. In a blazing sun, we drove away from my home on the Texas range land. The sand whispering beneath the buggy wheels was swirled into my eyes by the hot wind, giving me an excuse to wipe away the homesick tears and shield my face from the brand-new husband I scarcely knew and whom I still called Mr. Laune.

We were driving a team of beautifully matched horses, Harboldt and Broncho, hitched to the high-top buggy. Both horses were deep bay with long heavy black manes and tails and stocking feet. Each had a white star in the forehead between intelligent, wide-spaced eyes. Our way led through large cattle pastures covered with mesquite grass, and clumps of gray-green sagebrush. With the horses' feet skimming soundlessly over the springy sod, we drove mile after mile without benefit of roads. An occasional road runner would dart suddenly from the mesquite bushes and race ahead of us before slipping back into the grass where it was lost in the monotony of foliage. Jackrabbits, with their long black-tipped ears, leaped over the clumps of redtop and bluestem. A terrapin, waddling awkwardly, was sometimes accidentally kicked by the horses and overturned so its greenish yellow hinged floor was uppermost, and the small protruding feet and silly little tail waved impotently in the air.

I knew almost every foot of this land, having ridden over it alone and in company with Evelyn and our friends, the young men who worked the range. I told Mr. Laune of the let-down, an arrangement the fence-rider had made for me in the long Rockingchair pasture fence which I could manage without getting off my horse, when I was teaching in the Dozier and Indian Creek schools and made the trip back and forth to my home, a distance of some twenty miles, almost every week. One caution the men repeated to us girls over and over: "Never get off your horse when alone on the range. The horse might get away and leave you afoot. Cattle aren't accustomed to women, especially when they're wearing long trailing black riding-skirts. They're curious, and easily excited, then they're dangerous and might muss you up considerably."

We came at last to Salt Fork of Red River that flows through the Rockingchair. Like most western streams it trickled in a narrow flow for most of the year, moving lazily along its wide sandy bed. On one side the sand rippled and spread out over the prairies with no definite boundary, while on the other, red bluffs, deeply rutted with cattle trails leading down to the water, formed a high, steep bank.

Now Salt Fork was swollen with heavy summer rains, and the waters from the distant snow-covered mountains had deepened the channel and were rushing down the wide bed to Red River.

Harboldt and Broncho stood still while we watched the shallow water spreading out over the prairie. The moment they waded in I could feel the peculiar bumping that warned of quicksand. I was instantly on the alert and moved to the edge of the seat to look for a place on the other side where the horses could scramble up on dry land. In the washed-out channel the buggy swung downstream, but I breathed easily when I saw that the team recognized the danger and knew how to meet it.

At noon, we stopped for a lunch made from our wedding dinner—turkey and nutcake, I remember. We sat on the ground in the strip of shade cast by the buggy and ate and talked while the horses munched their oats from nosebags.

As he was measuring out the oats for the team Mr. Laune laughed and told me that when he bought them from the merchant in Wellington, a gangling youth wearing a large white Stetson hat, high-heeled boots, and tight Levis had strolled into the store and asked:

"How much is oats a pound, pleassir Mister?"

"Ten cents," snapped the merchant.

"Gimme two pounds, pleassir Mister."

The two pounds were weighed out in silence. Then,

"How much do I owe you, pleassir, Mister?"

"Thirty cents," grunted the merchant. Then seeing Mr. Laune's surprised glance, he muttered, "I charge him a dime for educating him, and it's cheap, at that."

Of course I knew Mr. Hamilton, the man who kept the store. He was a very dear friend of ours, the kindest person imaginable to those whom he liked, but I had cringed in sympathy many times for the victims of his caustic tongue.

We had not seen a human being since leaving my parents' home in the early morning. All around us lay the grassy plains dotted with white-faced cattle, while above us the sun blazed in the blue, blue sky. We sat with our backs to the wind that snatched at my hat, tied down with the usual thick veil. Meadow larks spilled their brief melody as they rose in the air. Cottontails peeped and dodged through the sagebrush. Horned toads slipped through the grass, and we scratched their rough spiny backs with small sticks and sifted hot sand over them as they lay with half-opened mouths and softly heaving sides.

We had had so few chances to sit alone and talk. We knew so little about each other. The only thing I really knew about this man whom I had married was that he took tender, loving care of his horses.

I said so, rather shyly, adding that it would be nice to know something more about him. We both laughed, it sounded so absurd under the circumstances.

"Where shall I start," he said. "*Not* with what a cunning baby I was, please."

"No," I agreed, thinking I'd hear about all that from his mother. "From about high school," I decided after a moment. "And don't leave anything out."

He drew a deep breath. "All right. Here we go on the autobiography of Sidney B. Laune. . . ."

And this is what he told me as we sat resting on the plains on our wedding day.

"After finishing high school I was unwilling to go to the University, almost next door to us in Lincoln, so Father took me into the office with him, where he did a law, real estate, loan and banking business. When I was about nineteen I suggested that my services rated a higher salary than he was paying me." He chuckled. "Father said that if I ever expected to be worth my salt, it was high time I demonstrated some ability along the line of self-development.

"That made me pretty darned sore. Here I was, practically taking care of the old-folks-at-home, in my estimation. 'What would you do without me, if I should leave you?' I asked Father, coldly.

" 'Oh, I should worry along,' he replied cheerfully. I was scandalized. Here was gratitude for you. I was sacrificing the best years of my life, staying at home with my old father and mother (they were in their forties). 'All right,' I said haughtily, 'I'll leave.'

"I really thought they would fall upon me with loud cries of anguish and beg me to remain with them, but instead, they began to help me make plans to leave. Father had some literature in the office about Colorado. It sounded pretty far away, although it was practically next door to Nebraska. I announced that I would go a-w-a-y out there and take land. Same old pioneer Go-West-Young-Man formula that my parents had used. So, I went to Colorado. I didn't know what I would do about not being twenty-one, but decided to file on land as 'head of the family.'

"I drove a team of mismatched horses to a rickety old wagon." He flipped a fly from Broncho's back and gave his low, quiet chuckle. "That team was a sight. Clipper, whose ancestors had raced over the western plains, was my riding pony, a small, stocky sorrel. He was quick and an honest worker, broken to harness as well as saddle. It was a shame to harness him with Deaver, a tall rangy bay with no great intelligence, wall-eyed, slow, with a mean disposition and given to balking. With this team, a breaking-plow, chuckbox, a trunk filled with books, tools, a wood-burning cookstove, canvas cot, and an assortment of other things I thought I might need, I started out."

He smiled at me after a moment's silent thought. "I'll bet Columbus's ideas about the discovery of America were no vaguer than mine. I knew one thing, I was going to stop before I got to the Rocky Mountains. I had to have room enough to breathe and wave my arms without danger of knocking off a few peaks here and there. And I knew I wouldn't be able to breathe all hedged in by mountains. I was prairie-born and prairie-bred, I had to have room in which to expand." He motioned with the whip where all around lay the expanse of flat land. "Like this.

"When I got to the country I had decided upon, I couldn't make up my mind which place to take. I wanted the whole region, and decided to take whatever the law would allow: a homestead, a tree-claim, a pre-emption, or a desert-claim. But, which? I rode miles trying to settle the question; anyway, I didn't know for sure what all those terms meant. Well"—he sighed and moved restlessly in the shade, stretching his long legs—"I went to the land office, and filled out the papers. Then I worked like a galley slave, fulfilling the demands required to hold the land, and later, prove up."

His face had grown stern and grim and his eyes narrowed in memory of those hard years.

"It was just when I thought I'd have to give up that, through a kind Providence, I met Paul B. Godsman. He was older than I, a doctor, and oddly enough, also a lawyer. I was blessed with his friendship. And after a time a railroad was built across the country and a small town was started near my land. Doctor Godsman and I started a drugstore. He taught me to render a number of unaccustomed and unrelated services. I was elected justice of the peace, and performed marriage ceremonies, sold real estate, and acted as counsel in legal matters. During an average day I might pull a tooth, assist the doctor in minor operations, sell drugs, marry a couple, make out filing papers, and sell a parcel of land. We promised to name our first sons for each other. Our son will be named Paul." He turned to look at me, and smiled, "Do you like that name?"

"I think it's a splendid name," I said.

He seemed pleased. "It was after Godsman's marriage that I knew I ought to have more education. I talked it over with him and he did what my parents had failed to do—convinced me that I should go to college. So I wrote Father and asked him if he would take a mortgage on the land I had acquired and let me have the money for college. He was most generous and I went to the Wesleyan University in Ohio where I got my B.S. degree. After that I went to Ann Arbor, Michigan, for my law degree. I then went to Denver to begin my practice. By that time I wasn't affected by mountains or anything else in the world, I knew I could just push them aside. I opened an office"—he shook with laughter—"office, in a pig's eye! I mean, I had desk room in the office of an old established firm of lawyers.

"Just about the time that I had my nice new swivel chair tipped back and my feet on my shiny new desk, the bottom fell out of the world. Banks failed all over the country. The panic of 1893 swept the United States, and bread lines formed in Denver.

"And then Uncle Sam came to the rescue: he opened the Cherokee Strip for settlement. I read about it, and one night walked into a meeting that was being held in a downtown hall. I was just in time for some sort of election; I didn't know what. I sat down and a man who was next to me whispered: 'What's your name?' I whispered back: 'Sidney Laune.' He jumped to his feet and hollered: 'I nominate Sidney Laune!' Someone shouted: 'I second the nomination,' and someone else called out: 'I move the nominations be closed.' This was voted on and I found myself the secretary of the Denver-Cherokee Outlet Colony. Later, through some other circumstances, I became the president of the Colony.

"There certainly wasn't any business in the city of Denver for a young lawyer just beginning to practice, so I thought I'd join this Colony and try my luck in the new country. It has proved to be a happy decision. I brought the Denver-Cherokee Outlet Colony from Colorado and we drove our stakes in what was called East Woodward. The location was contested by a man who wanted that particular place for a homestead, but after representing the contest by the Colony, we have won the case through all the courts and are awaiting the final decision by the Department of the Interior. It's all sewed up in our favor."

He turned to me with a smile. "Is that what you wanted?"

I nodded. He had, I knew, left out a great deal, but I also knew I would learn it all in the years to come. The sun had passed the meridian and the little haven of shade shifted. The wind blew spitefully and the sand swirled into our eyes and food. Mr. Laune moved closer to me. Sunlight caught the back of his head and one ear seemed to be on fire. He paid little attention to the wind and sun, and I think I saw him with my mind for the first time. I noticed how white his skin was above his cuffs; how tanned his face and hands. I realized how gentle was his voice and how beautifully his lips were curved.

For a long while we sat silent, his blue-gray eyes squinted as he looked out over the high, sage-dotted grassy plain. I think he had forgotten me. "Beautiful land," he murmured as though talking to himself. "What a paradise it would be if we could conserve and control the storm waters that we so desperately need for crops and stock. Water would make this land a garden of plenty.

"If the people," he turned to me, "would build dams across the draws and make a lake on every farm and ranch, the water could be kept at home and be used for irrigation and reservoirs. If everyone would plant trees! I'm a tree planter, a Nebraskan." He laughed as he patted my knee and looked around at the tree-less prairie, and raised his eyes to the blue sky that reached down to the land and was tucked in neatly around the edge of the prairies. "Do you like this country?" he asked me. Then, anxiously, "Do you?"

"Oh yes," I replied, breathlessly, fighting the words out past the lump in my throat, "I love it, I can't bear to leave it."

After another silence in which I thought I was again forgotten, he said, "You have the darnedest name! Where did you get it? Did your mother read a book? I doubt I shall ever learn to pronounce it, and I don't for the life of me know how to spell it. What am I going to call you?"

"It came from a great-grandmother in Virginia. It was my grandmother's name, too. I like it; maybe because I was so fond of my grandmother and felt so honored to be named for her."

"Well, let's see. Your mother called you Nonie; your father leaves out the i, and calls you None, when he doesn't call you Scamp; the children call you Sister. I'll be darned if I'm going to continue to call my wife, Miss Nonie. And are you, for heaven's sake, going to call me Mr. Laune?" He mimicked me. "Suppose you practice saying Sidney. That's my name, you know."

I said it. "Sidney." He gave one of his rare shouts of merriment.

"That," he said, "was the most unconvincing squeak I ever heard. Can't you do better than that? Suppose you go on practicing while I hitch up the horses."

We drove until after ten o'clock that night, over dim roads and no roads, but the ranch house where, on his way over, Mr. Laune had arranged for us to stay, was tucked away in some far draw perhaps; anyway, we couldn't find it.

The sky was white with stars and moonlight. As usual, at the setting of the sun the wind died down to a caressing murmur, patting the earth that it had harassed all day, tenderly, repentantly. The sand no longer stung our cheeks and eyes. Rabbits leaped and frolicked in the white light, and a chorus of coyotes rang through the still air.

The horses showed signs of weariness, and plodded along with drooping heads. Mr. Laune sang, " 'Where the moon rides high, and the stars swing low,' " but I was too worn out to sing. He asked in a troubled voice, "Getting pretty tired, aren't you?"

I nodded. I knew he must be as tired as I, but was reluctant to suggest spending the night on the prairie. I saw no sense in rambling along under the July stars all night searching for some hidden ranch house. I said, "Let's stop."

He explained in embarrassment what I already knew; that we were not equipped for camping. But after a moment's hesitation, he helped me from the buggy, tossed out the cushion and buggy robes, and began unhitching the horses. Before he had finished picketing the team out, I was asleep.

The next morning when the sun streamed into my face, I saw how luxuriously I was bedded between the robes on a fragrant pile of sagebrush he had cut with his pocketknife and formed into a mound. I could scarcely remember when I had crept into this comfortable bed and pillowed my head on his shoulder.

The horses were already hitched to the buggy when I opened my eyes. Mr. Laune was sitting inside, with his hat tipped to shade his face while he waited for me to waken. As soon as I stirred, he came to greet me.

"Your bath, my lady, is waiting."

He folded the robes and returned the cushion while I straightened out the wrinkles in my clothes. We drove to the creek he

stable and we started out to see for ourselves. Everyone with whom he talked told us, with varying expressions of polite profanity, that we could not cross the river. Several of the cowboys mounted their ponies and rode beside us as we drove down to look the situation over.

Like all the other streams, the South Canadian was but a narrow flow for most of the year, moving lazily between sandy banks. But after the thawing of the mountain snows and the downpour of summer storms had emptied their toll into the various tributaries, creeks, draws, and arroyos, it became a raging torrent.

As we drew near it, we heard the snarling growl of rushing water, and saw a great sea spread out before us. Mr. Laune gave me a grim smile. "Well, there she is," he said, "living up to her best tradition."

He stopped the horses and we sat and watched while the cowboys reined in beside us. My prairie eyes had never seen so much water.

"Gol-lee," yelled one of the men sitting with one leg thrown over the pommel of his saddle, "look at 'er roll! It'd be mighty unhealthy, Mister, to jump into that gravy. It'd sure be sudden death." Pretty soon the men turned their ponies back toward town, shouting above the roar of water, "See you at sundown, Mister."

"How about it?" Mr. Laune asked me, quietly, "Shall we risk it? Or go back to the hotel and wait until tomorrow, when it might go down?"

I was amazed that he thought we had any choice, gruesome as the idea of going back to that hotel might be. I stared at the tumbling water, roiled with boiling sand.

"The horses are western bred and know quicksand. They're well broken and reliable. They know their business; they're obedient and intelligent." He spoke firmly, as though to convince himself.

"What would you do if you were alone?" I asked.

The sound of the water was almost deafening. He sat with eyes squinted and lips pressed together. "I—I don't know. Jump in, I suppose. But having you with me makes me hesitate. I really don't want to drown you—yet." He grinned. Then he asked, "Can you swim?"

I shook my head, remembering that for five years I had not seen much more than a pitcher of water at a time, let alone enough to swim in. And I'm like a cat about getting wet; I hate it. I didn't even like to wade in a stream. I had lived on the prairies too long for that.

Mr. Laune turned to me again. "Well?"

I drew a deep breath. "All right, I'm not afraid," I lied.

"It's risky," he said. "You're sure you are not afraid?"

"I'm not afraid," I repeated between stiff lips. That was my story, and I was going to stay by it if it killed me; and I thought it would.

He got out of the buggy and explained that the quicksand in the South Canadian was not as quick as in some streams. I took that statement with a barrel of salt. He pointed to some trees far out in the ocean, waving their branches pitifully, as though signaling for help.

"There's a little island there, and the horses can get a moment's breathing spell."

For an hour we prepared for the plunge, hoping that the water would go down a little. We tied the suitcases, hatbox and robes on top of the buggy. Mr. Laune strengthened and made rigid the braces that supported the top so it wouldn't buckle or collapse. He took off his shoes and rolled his trousers above his knees and stuck a knife in his belt. Then he said:

"Now listen. I want you to sit up on the back of the buggy seat. Brace your feet on the cushion, lean forward, and hold on to the brace." I obeyed. "Now, listen carefully," he repeated, and patted my feet as he settled himself beside them. "If I see that the horses can't make it, or if anything happens that requires it, I shall cut them loose from the buggy, first. Don't move until I tell you to. We may have to tail the horses in. The buggy will ride like a boat unless it is washed about too suddenly and something breaks. It's loaded pretty heavy on the top, but I can't help that. All ready? Remember, if I see the horses are unable to buck the tide, I'll cut them loose first, and take care of you later. Understand? Let's go."

I couldn't help smiling to myself, though my stomach was shaking. Horses first, of course; but I nodded.

He sat forward, tense and alert, gathered up the lines, poised the whip over the horses' backs, and spoke quietly: "All right, boys, wade in."

For a few feet the horses sloshed along in the fast-flowing, thick, sandy, water. Suddenly, they dropped where the channel deepened. The buggy swerved downstream with a creak of straining tongue and singletrees. I thought for an awful moment that our crossing was over before it had begun. But everything held and the horses swam for a moment with great lunging strokes, their noses just above the swirling water.

Mr. Laune called encouragement to them, and they found footing and bumped along, the water pouring through the buggy. The whip touched each gleaming back in rhythm to the chant shouted above the churning water: "Steady boys! *On*, Harboldt. *On*, Broncho. *Good* boys. *All* right. *Go* on."

The confident voice of praise beat time to the touch of the whip, to the roar of the water, to the groaning and grunting of the team. My ears sang and, dizzy with watching the rushing stream, I almost toppled from my perch.

In places where the water was less deep, the quivering and bumping beneath us told of quicksand which seemed to me as quick as any I had ever encountered.

Again we dropped where the channel had cut deep and the water eddied in a circle. My stomach flopped uncertainly. The buggy squealed and complained and again swept downstream with sickening suddenness. I sat so light that my weight must have counted for nothing. The horses swam, breathing gustily and groaningly, found footing, and after an eternity reached the spot where the trees were waving their arms, and pulled up to rest a moment. They puffed and blew, with heaving sides and flaring nostrils, but their heads were high and their eyes bright when they turned questioningly toward us.

Mr. Laune crept between them along the buggy tongue and examined belts, buckles and straps; patted their rumps, their sides, and lifted collars and backbands. He ran gentle hands along their dripping necks, fondled their ears, and brushed back their manes and forelocks, arranging their browbands. All the while, he kept telling them how wonderful they were, and how proud he was of them.

I stretched my stiff neck and shoulders as he eased into his seat again, tightened the reins and laid the whip along the horses' backs. Their ears pointed forward, the whip tapped. "All right boys, wade in."

We were about halfway across. A wide, reddish gray waste lay before us. I wanted desperately to stay there in the shallower water near the trees.

My ears sang and the sunlight on the water made me sick at my stomach, and the strange queasy feeling threatened to dislodge me from my uncomfortable perch. But I had been cautioned not to move. I held hard to the brace and the back of the seat.

Just as I would decide that the going was safe at last, and I could breathe again, the horses would drop. Eight hooves would pack sand, keeping time to the pounding of my heart. Never plunging, never floundering, their steady limbs met every demand made upon their strength. Then again, the shallower water and the quivering sand . . .

At last we drove out over the top of a four-strand barbed-wire fence which the sand had covered. I had not spoken or made a single sound. Now I was sure I would disgrace myself and cry.

But Mr. Laune gave an exultant laugh, patted my wet feet, and sprang from the buggy. He stripped the harness from the horses and rubbed them down with handfuls of sagebrush. Trying to straighten my spine and neck, I staggered to the ground.

He caught me to him and we looked back over that angry red sea. Moses' tribe could not have been more awed at their crossing than we were at the miracle we had experienced.

He stood with his arms around me. "I wouldn't drive into that river again for ten thousand dollars," he declared solemnly. "A man would be an unmitigated fool to risk his life like that."

Wet, but jubilant, we drove through the rough pasture until we came to a windmill where an old man was watering stock from the tank beside it.

"Canadian's sure on a bender," he croaked. "A swallow couldn't cross it. Th'ain't any use goin' any closter, Mister, y'can't cross it today, ner tomorrow, neither."

"We just crossed it," Mr. Laune replied. There was no pride in his voice; just wonder and unbelief.

The old man eyed us irritably. "I said," he shouted, "y'can't cross the river today."

After we had convinced him that we actually had driven through those wild waters, he turned on us in a fury. "What you done," he yelled, "that you're runnin' away from? Is the law after you, or a pappy with a gun?"

We left him muttering angrily, undecided whether he should report us as criminals, runaway lovers, or merely lunatics.

We reached the Black Ranch on Turkey Creek that evening in time for a late supper, and did not hurry away next morning. Great cottonwood trees grew along the creek that ran near the house, where squirrels could be seen playing in and out among the branches. Mockingbirds sang and jaybirds scolded and I saw an oriole. It had been a long time since I had seen birds that nested in trees. Our Texas varieties, the meadow larks, road runners, killdeers, and doves, all birds of the prairies, made their nests on the ground. I loved them, but the tree-nesting birds were different and their songs more exuberant.

I was reluctant to leave, because I knew that when we reached Woodward and the railroad, we would take the train for Nebraska; and Nebraska seemed as far away from my Texas home and my loved ones as the moon.

We were now in more settled country and saw more claim shanties and ranch houses. The sky was studded with stars, and the moon rode high that night when Mr. Laune stopped the team

on a hill and pointed with his whip. A cluster of lights glimmered in the valley below.

"There she is," he said proudly. "There's Woodward."

We drove to the Central Hotel, and Mr. Laune registered: "Mr. and Mrs. Sidney B. Laune," the first time I had seen my new name written.

No one in the town, except his partner, Judge Dean, had ever heard of me, or knew of Mr. Laune's intention to be married. There was quite a commotion in the lobby after the clerk's excited exclamation. The men from the bar next door crowded around us to be introduced, shake hands, and extend their congratulations and good wishes.

I knew that Temple Houston, who had entered Woodward from Higgins, Texas, on the same train with Mr. Laune and his Colony, was living in the town, and he greeted me as "a fellow-Texan."

Everyone who has ever lived in Texas soon learns Texas history and the part General Sam Houston played in its foundation and subsequent development. No one regards the Houston family with indifference. Nor was Temple Houston regarded indifferently in Woodward.

He was a handsome man, tall and straight, with searching eyes. As I placed my hand in his I felt an instant liking. His manner was quick and nervous. He walked with short jerky steps, the exaggerated flare of his bell-bottom trousers flapping about his small, high-heeled boots. He spoke in the same quick, nervous way, except on occasions when his voice fell to a slow deliberate drawl, hardly above a whisper. Every word and movement represented drama.

As he stood with my hand in his, he teased me about my husband whom he often opposed in legal battles. The crowd drew closer, for Temple Houston was a master storyteller, and there was the added incentive in the jibing directed toward the newly married man before his bride. The fact that we might be tired did not seem to occur to him, or to the delighted group around

us, as he recounted with relish the story of the time he and
Mr. Laune were returning from Beaver City, where they had
gone on the District Court circuit; Mr. Laune was driving a new
team of bronchos to his buggy.

"I was impatient to get home," said Mr. Houston, "but Laune
was determined to give his horses the consideration he thought
due them." (I smiled at that.) "The weather was hot," Mr.
Houston went on, "and the way over the almost unmarked prairie was long and monotonous. I kept telling Laune it was important for me to get to Woodward as soon as possible, but he
refused to hurry the horses.

"Noon came, and I was nodding in my seat when Laune
stopped the team and began to unhitch them from the buggy. I
sat up and remonstrated in fervid eloquence, but to no purpose.
Laune hung nosebags from their ears and never did two animals
take more time to munch their grain. Then, gentlemen"—as the
crowd around us pushed and laughed his voice fell into his deepest courtroom tone—"heaven help me, if he didn't start to picket
them out to graze! He said they were too tired to continue the
journey without rest. After expending my breath in futile argument, I stretched out on the prairie sod, pulled my hat over my
brow, and prepared to sleep.

"Suddenly, there was the most frightful ripping and snorting.
I looked up to see those poor weary animals that needed refresh-
ment and rest, tearing over the peaceful landscape as though all—"
he bowed and grinned at me—"the furies of Hades were driving
them.

"S. B. was standing there with a hurt, baffled look on his face,
watching them go. Helter-skelter, with harness flying, they high-
tailed it into the far blue distance.

"And I said," Mr. Houston twisted the long forelock that hung
over his forehead and gritted his teeth in what I later knew was
his characteristic gesture when angry, "I said, I hope to God
those poor jaded beasts get some rest and grass! Then I closed
my eyes and went back to sleep." The men roared and nudged
each other. "While I slept there in the shade of the buggy, S. B.

trudged over the prairie, through the blistering heat, after those da-durned horses. He caught them somewhere cornered in a pasture, or they'd be running yet."

At last Mr. Laune went to put the horses in their own little stable and Mrs. L. B. Collins, who with her husband kept the hotel, showed me to our room. I was tired and hot, and wanted a more adequate bath than the flowered bowl and pitcher in our room could supply so Mrs. Collins offered to heat a kettle of water and let me have the use of a tub.

As the water was heating, she told me of her first bath in the town. She and her husband had come in the day of the Run, and staked the claim where the hotel stood. They did not come together as they thought their chances for securing the location they wanted might be better if they acted independently. They were prepared with tents and equipment necessary for starting an eating-place to feed the hungry horde that they knew would swarm in after the signal was given. Mrs. Collins was such a dignified, refined little lady that it was hard to imagine her struggling with the task of feeding the mob that rushed into the tent almost as soon as it was pegged to the ground. Perhaps her quiet, gentle dignity was the secret of their success through the years that followed that hectic day on September 16, 1893.

After two days and nights, during which she could not rest or even undress, she was in a state of physical, mental and emotional collapse. Her husband, almost as tired as she, tried to think of something he could do to give her some rest before it was time to prepare the next meal.

"If I could only have a bath and some fresh clothes," she wailed, as they sat together in the hot dining tent.

"A bath?" he repeated drearily. "Where could you take a bath, even if we could spare the water?" All they had was a whiskey barrelful filled from a water wagon that hauled water in from the springs two miles out of town. That water was more precious than rubies. It had to be guarded jealously, and conserved for drinking and cooking. Of course, it could not be used for bathing, even if one could find the privacy for such an intimate ceremony.

"After a while," she told me, "L. B. rose and hurried out of the tent. When he returned, victory was in his eyes.

" 'Get everything ready, you're going to have a bath,' he announced. 'Get your soap, towels, and clean clothes, and hurry!' "

She stopped to laugh. "It was like pulling a white rabbit out of a silk hat; but L. B. had never failed me, and I knew he would not this time.

"We got into a wagon that L. B. hired on the street and he ordered the driver to take us to the river, about a mile north of town. After we reached the river, L. B. dismissed the driver with the promise to return for us in about an hour.

"There wasn't even so much as a cactus leaf to hide behind, but after looking around we found a sheltering bank. At least, it was a shelter on two sides; the other sides opened out for miles in sight of anyone who came that way.

" 'Get behind that bank, and I'll stand guard,' L. B. told me. 'We have an hour, so don't hurry. After you're through, I'll get in and you can keep watch.'

"Of course, I was nervous and hurried at first; but we were really as private as though we were in a closet with the door locked. After a few minutes, I relaxed and stretched out in the shallow water and almost went to sleep. It was wonderful. Then, all nice and fresh and clean, I sat on the bank and rested while L. B. bathed. We went there every day after that until we got the hotel built."

In 1896 Woodward, not yet three years old, was a typical Western town. It was built along one wide Main Street, instead of around a "square" as were our small Texas towns. Houses were scattered here and there with little regard for any ordered plan. There were no trees, except a small cottonwood grove near the railroad property. Sand blew in ripples along the street. People hurried along in pleasant activity, and it seemed to me every one of them stopped to speak to Mr. Laune and express their sympathy at the death of his father, and exclaim in surprise when I was introduced. The morning sun beat down, cracking and drying the edge of the mud puddle in front of the bank and drug-

store, but it had been so long since I had seen so large a town that everything looked wonderful to me.

We started at once from the hotel to see Judge Dean.

Judge Dean reminded me of my father, though some years older. From the moment I saw him, all through the years until his death, I loved and admired him. He had not yet brought his family from Texas, and he and Mr. Laune had lived together.

Perhaps it was no accident that the two men had secured lots adjoining each other the day of the Run. They had opened their respective "offices" by the simple process of taking from their suitcases their office supplies, consisting of some legal blanks, and then sitting on their suitcases and waiting for business.

They formed an agreement for mutual protection of their claims; while one was away for trips to the land office, or to get food, or some other necessity, the other would stand guard. That was a great convenience, but what about the business? The man on the ground got that. So a short time later a neatly lettered sign, "Dean and Laune, Lawyers," was nailed to a stake driven into the line separating the two lots.

As we walked from the hotel to the office I had noticed a curve, a decided bend in the long Main Street. While Mr. Laune was busy packing boxes, typewriter, and other things to ship to Nebraska, I asked Judge Dean about this curve.

He assumed a troubled air, and replied solemnly, "There are people who say that Dean and Laune are so crooked that they have actually caused the street to bend near their office. We think they're a l-e-e-tle mite prejudiced, don't we, S. B.?"

Mr. Laune went on packing and did not look up. I began to worry.

"Do people think that?" I asked.

Then Mr. Laune said, mildly, "That's where East and West Woodward merge. East Woodward is the part of town that's in litigation. The Judge and I are representing it, and that's where I, and the Colony I brought from Denver, settled. It was platted to conform with the Sante Fe Railroad. Whereas West Woodward, the town platted by the government before the Opening,

We sat in silence, while I watched the wagons, buggies, and horseback riders trotting up and down the street. I thought of that first Sunday School, and wished we were not leaving this nice town.

But now the packing was finished and we got ready to leave. Judge Dean stood tall and straight as we shook hands, and he gave Mr. Laune a lingering pat on the shoulder. "You'll come back, son, when you've finished that Nebraska chore? I'll watch out for things here."

Right from the first I loved the people and the little town of Milford, Nebraska. Most of the inhabitants were elderly couples who had retired from business or moved in from their farms after their children had married and gone away. They puttered among their gardens and flowers or sat in the shade of the trees in their yards and read, crocheted, or napped.

No one thought of calling the wives of the Laune boys "Mrs. Laune." Mother was the only Mrs. Laune. We were Mrs. Cassius, Mrs. Finley, and now, Mrs. Sidney. People thought it was amusing that I called my husband Mr. Laune, but it seemed perfectly natural to me. My mother called Father, Mr. Russell. My grandmother had called my grandfather, Mr. West. I was taught to believe—though Mr. Laune said I forgot it with amazing rapidity—that a husband was the head of the house, and to be respected because he was older and, by reason of going to business and mingling with other men, wiser. It was a sort of ring-around-a-rosy process of reasoning, but it was never questioned in my family.

Brother Cash gave me a beautiful thoroughbred Kentucky gelding named Dexter for a wedding gift. Nothing could have pleased me more. As Mr. Laune was busy in the office, having been admitted to practice law in Nebraska, he had little time to ride with me, so I rode alone. The buggies and wagons, clogging the streets and roads, made it very different from tearing over the unrestricted Texas range. No one else in Milford rode horseback and I felt guilty riding aimlessly over the country when I should have been learning to cook and keep house.

Mr. Laune teased me about having married him under false pretenses. "I thought I was marrying a wonderful cook," he complained wistfully, "because you did make that cream-of-tomato soup, and that chocolate cake. I watched you do it."

"But that, and biscuits and cornbread, was all I knew how to cook," I explained, not sure whether he was joking or not.

"Don't worry, I'll teach you to cook," Mother promised comfortably. "Anyone can learn to cook if she can read, has a grain of common sense, and a spark of imagination. And," she added, "if she wants to. I'll start you off before I go to Colorado to visit Fin and Laura, and when I return you'll be a professional."

She gave me a cookbook, and I bought an account book.

"Here's one piece of advice for you," remarked my husband when he found me busy with pots and pans, while Dexter nickered lonesomely in the stable lot. "Never let household duties cheat you out of enjoyment. Pleasures are fleeting things, coming sometimes quickly and unexpectedly; and housework is like the poor, it's with you always."

He picked up the account book in which I had listed: *Sugar, 50¢; potatoes? rice?* "Good heavens," he breathed, "what are you doing with this?"

"Keeping account of what I spend," I replied virtuously.

He stared at me with growing displeasure. "Aw, now, honey, do we have to do that? Isn't it enough that we earn the money to spend without having to work ourselves to a nubbin to keep track of what we spend it for? I call that downright silly." He tore out the page and crumpled it in his hand. "We're neither of us going to be extravagant and spend more than we can afford, so let's not fret ourselves into gray hair about sugar and rice and then lie awake trying to remember what went with that two cents we can't account for."

Maybe in the years that followed he would have liked to eat those words, but, if so, he never mentioned it.

Soon after Mother went to Colorado, Mr. Laune came home and announced that he had accepted an invitation for us to attend the National Encampment of the Grand Army of the Republic. I had never heard of this organization, but I did know Captain Culver and his family, who were old friends of the Launes and had asked us to be their guests at the Encampment in Lincoln. I was delighted.

"Will it be a picnic?" I asked.

He grinned. "Something like that, I suspect."

It was like a picnic and a circus, with flags flying, and guidons and banners waving and fluttering from tents. Drums and fifes and bands were pounding and piping and blaring. The field was laid out like an army camp, with tents bordering orderly streets.

We ate in the mess hall with Captain and Mrs. Culver and their other guests, and went with them to listen to the speeches where I laughed and applauded and had a good time. For a while . . .

Presently, I felt my cheeks beginning to burn; and soon, I was getting mad. And madder. I didn't know about those battles of the Civil War that the speaker was talking about. But the things he was saying were certainly not complimentary to my folks back home. In the rural phrase: "That wasn't the way I heerd it."

I became especially enraged by a nice, quiet-looking old gentleman, General Somebody, who was telling about the Battle of Gettysburg. General Pickett and the Confederates he was leading were anything but shining heroes, according to the speaker. As I listened, I liked less and less the manner in which he referred to the Confederate Army. When he made slighting remarks about Robert E. Lee, I could not bear it. I was afraid all those people listening might believe what he said.

"Why, the old storyteller! What does he mean by talking like that? Why, he knows that's not true." I was muttering, not too softly, and almost crying, when I felt my fingers, that were doubled up into a tight-fisted knot, squeezed by my husband.

"Now, now," he whispered, grinning, "you needn't get all flustered and bothered. Let the old boy have his say. Remember, he was there, and he fought and bled and died for a cause that you have only heard about." The band began playing "America." "Aren't you glad it's all over, and that you can sing 'My Country

'Tis of Thee.' Of course you are, darned glad!

"Now, you just wait," he chuckled, "until the G.A.R.s and their wives and daughters, and grandchildren, 'fifty thousand strong,' sing: 'Marching Through Georgia.' That's a ditty you never heard, I'll bet, and it sure-enough will stir your red corpuscles."

"I want to go home." I sulked.

"No, you don't," he answered firmly, "you want to stay and hear the other side of the story of the 'late unpleasantness.' That man has something to tell you that you don't know. He may have a one-sided view too, but at least you will have heard his side."

After the speeches, as we sat in Captain Culver's tent, the speaker who had infuriated me was there, as well as a number of other notables, and we fought a kind of sequel to The War. I told them some of the things *I* had heard, but we parted friends, nevertheless.

So that I would not be lonely during Mother's absence, Mr. Laune gave me two coons that he bought from a boy who had caught them on the creek. He thought they would be nice pets and give me an interesting diversion, he said.

I was not fooled. I knew he bought them for his own interesting diversion, so I said nothing of my aversion. I thought that would be shockingly selfish.

I was scared to pieces of those coons, and they knew it, but I was ashamed to tell Mr. Laune. When he started to train Jack and Jenny, as he called them, I watched the proceedings from the safety of the middle of the dining-room table. I explained that I took this position so I would be out of the way.

The coons were smart, and learned to do a number of cunning tricks. They learned to wrestle with each other and with Rowdy, Mother's small shaggy dog. There were rules that regulated these wrestling matches. No rough stuff, like biting, snapping, snarling and scratching. They seemed to understand Mr. Laune's commands, for almost immediately, at his command, they would stand up again, wrap their arms and legs around each other, and sway and push and strain, until they fell in a furry heap on the floor. But when I spoke to them with what I thought was a note of authority, they swished their bushy tails and twisted their rear ends in insulting disregard.

The young men of the town would come and watch these matches with whoops of laughter. We held almost nightly sessions of coon-training. Rowdy entered into the skirmishes with indifference, but he was a well-mannered little dog and had been taught to obey; however, you could tell that the coons were not his best friends.

When Jack and Jenny were engaged in the arena, Rowdy would watch the contest from the safe pillow in the Boston rocker. Jack, the smarter, more engaging of the two, would, during the rest period between his tussles with Jenny, creep under the chair and tweak Rowdy's tail hanging through the open arm. Rowdy would whirl around angrily and peep down to see his tormentor. His tail would then hang down on the other side, and Jack, lying on his back, seemed to grin slyly, and would tweak Rowdy's tail on that side. Again, Rowdy would flounce around, and again, his tail would be pulled.

Though Mr. Laune chained the coons in the yard, they were constantly slipping their small wedge-shaped heads through their collars and gaining entrance to the house. Once inside, they raced upstairs and down, while I impotently shouted orders.

On one occasion I was munching a dill pickle while wandering among the cedars in the yard. As I passed the coons snoozing in front of their kennel they reared up on their hind legs and began to beg. I held out the pickle and Jack snatched it from my fingers. He gave it an inquisitive smell, shuddered, laid it down as if he expected it to explode in his face, and retreated to the dark of the kennel.

After a while, he crept out, approached the pickle cautiously, smelled it, shivered, turned it over and took an investigating nibble. I laughed out loud at the squeak of surprise and the startled look on his usually smug little face. He laid the strange thing down very gently and crawled back into the safe darkness. In a little while he came out again, and the whole performance was repeated until the pickle was consumed.

Mr. Laune had sent to Ohio for maple syrup that he thought superlative, but after it came he noticed that I did not eat it with enthusiasm.

"What's the matter, don't you like maple syrup?" he asked in disappointment.

"Yes, I like it," I answered without much conviction.

"What kind of syrup do you like best?"

"Well, I like sugar-house best, a syrup that's made in open kettles on the plantations in the South. There's never enough for commercial use, though. Next, I like sorghum."

"Sorghum, for heaven's sake!"

"Mm-hm. The kind the Capertons make at home."

"I see. Well, you shall have sorghum; but the kind the Amish make in Seward County."

So we drove out into the country to Mr. Stauffer's and got a gallon or two of sorghum which we brought home in a wicker-covered demijohn and put on the pantry floor.

One morning, after working and singing happily in the kitchen while I prepared our noon dinner, I dressed the table in our prettiest linen, china, and silver. Our very own things, not Mother's. I put the dinner on the table and ran down the walk to meet Mr. Laune and escort him to the table. When we entered the room, we were paralyzed by a vision of havoc and destruction. Jack and Jenny sat in the middle of the table. The cute little round roast that had received such gentle care in cooking, was nestled cozily within the circle of Jack's legs. Rice and gravy were mixed in a puddle through which Jenny swished her furry tail when she saw us. The water glasses were overturned. Everything on the table was in one horrid mess.

For a moment my anger overcame my fear and I started for those coons with murder in my heart. But they bared their teeth at me and stood up to do battle. Jenny, the hussy, chattered defiantly.

When I reached Memphis, Texas, I found the mail-hack waiting at the station for me. The familiar wind scudded across the prairie, snatching the words from my mouth, and yanking my hat from my head. It took joyous flight, like a pigeon released from a strange loft. Ezra McDowell was driving the mail that day, and gave chase, coming back panting and whipping the sand from my beautiful hat against his pants leg.

I could not take my eyes from the broad sweep of land. I asked Ez about my family. He replied, hesitantly, that Father was looking frail. "I'm sure glad you're home again, Miss Nonie, because Mrs. Russell doesn't look too good, either. It hasn't seemed right, with you away. The kids are all right. I reckon your folks'll almost lose their minds to have you back. And I wouldn't be surprised if the kids meet us at Buck Creek. I'll bet Professor Russell and your mother have had their opera glasses trained on the road all morning."

He was right. Fritz and Fan, both riding my pony, Jim, came galloping up the sandy road yelling their welcome. When they reached the hack, tears were streaming down Fan's face. They could not wait for Ezra to stop but rode up beside us and nearly dragged me from my seat. Fan scrambled from Jim's back and remained in the hack beside me, while Fritz kept close beside us as Jim swung along in the easy gait to which Father had trained him.

After the first shock of seeing the change that illness and worry had made in my parents, I settled down happily in my old place, with Father saying each night: "Nine o'clock, Scamp, put out the light and go to bed."

"I'm writing to Mr. Laune. Can't I finish?"

"Plenty of time in the morning. Light out, now."

And I would obey.

Each day, I saddled Jim and went for long rides over the green land. Mama would caution, "Be careful, dear. Ride slowly. Remember, you mustn't race and jump the draws as you used to do, before—"

I would promise, but as soon as Jim felt the tightening of the reins he would shake his head, give a few dancing steps, and we would be off, the wind singing in my ears. But we did not jump the draws.

The first of May, Mama sent for Mary. She had two babies, and it seemed odd for her to be so burdened with responsibilties. Mary was immediately conscious of the gravity of Father's condition and tried to make me see it. But he dressed carefully each morning, drawing about his tall slender form the red silk sash of his dark blue, red-embroidered dressing gown, and twice each day when the mail came he was at his desk to receive it. Then back to the couch, with the drawers beneath that opened out on either side and held his books, papers, and the knitting with which he busied himself.

We all found amusement in Father's knitting. After he became confined to the house, he said to Mama, "When I was a child, I broke my leg. During the weeks I lay in bed, my mother taught me to knit. I wonder if I remember how."

He sent to Kansas City for needles and yarn and spent many hours knitting warm stockings, gloves, wristlets, and comforters for the children and friends on the range.

While he knitted, we would talk. We would talk about Mr. Laune, whom he loved and admired, about me and my duties as a wife and as mother of the expected child. Sometimes he would refer casually to the time when we might have to manage without his guiding hand. But he had been frail for so long and had always been so careful to shield us from any unhappiness, I refused to admit to myself that there was any alarming change. I was simply incapable of imagining life without him.

Not until that last week, after Mary came, was he willing to remain in bed. Even then, the two children, Fritz, twelve, and Fan, eight, carried on an amazing amount of work under his direction. They seemed to rejoice in doing things that children are seldom able to manage. They would come flying to Father and sit on the side of the bed to receive instructions and praise. It seemed that he directed every single task on the place.

"What are you doing?" he called to me as he rapped on the partition wall one morning, while I was busy tidying the pantry shelves. "Stop that now, and come and sit beside me for a while."

After we had talked for some time he said, "Call your mother, then go to your room and don't come back until you are called. Try to take a nap. It's so hot, you should rest more." He pulled me down and kissed me as I unsuspectingly rose to obey him.

Mama had sent for Mrs. McDowell. I could hear her and my sister and Mama talking and hurrying about as I lay on my bed looking out over the sun-drenched land. The sky was stretched tight above the earth and the heat-devils danced above the grass.

I may have slept, for I felt Mrs. McDowell's hand on my shoulder as she sat down on the bed beside me. When I smiled up at her, she said:

"Your father has gone, Miss Nonie."

"Gone?" For a moment I could not comprehend what she said. I could not believe that she meant my father was dead. I started to spring to my feet and go to him. She pushed me back and placed her hand firmly on my arm. "Lie still," she commanded, "your mother is with him. Leave her alone now."

I could hear my sister in the hall, heartbreak in her voice, as she talked soothingly to her fretful babies.

"But I was just talking to him, I just left him," I sobbed. "He can't be gone."

"Where are Fritz and Fan?" I cried. Fritz and Fran were almost a compound word, so constantly were they together. I found them in the barn, but they were not together. Fritz was hiding behind a rick of fodder, his face buried in his arms, his body shaking with the sobs he tried to muffle. Fan, huddled down in a manger, was weeping softly. Both children were trying to bear this first grief alone. How could they know how to bear it so bravely?

We found on Father's desk the letters and telegrams he had written, in which he had left blank spaces for the hour and day of his death, with instructions for us to fill them in. He had written the necessary letters regarding his insurance, and had made all arrangements with the undertaker in Memphis. He had done everything he could to relieve us of all sudden, imperative duties.

What would we do without him? To whom would we go to talk over our hopes, our aims, and our perplexities? Whom could we ask— Where is Afghanistan? How do you square a circle? When was the Spanish Inquisition? What does, *Une fois n'est pas coutume,* mean? Oh, what would we do without him?

Though he had left so many explicit instructions for us to follow, Father had also talked long and intimately with Uncle Ed, who lived about five miles from us. I was thinking, Fritz will have to go for Uncle Ed, when he walked into the house.

Father's body was sent back to Little Rock, alone. Mama insisted that she could not and would not leave us.

The day after his death we watched the casket borne away over the prairie in the light spring-wagon driven by the undertaker. Uncle Ed rode his horse beside it.

There were probably friends there besides the McDowells and Bonners, and the sun was most certainly shining, but my memory holds a day of darkness and bitter grief with those two groups of friends beside us, as we huddled in the doorway watching as long as we could see it, the wagon with the casket, and Uncle Ed, moving slowly away in the distance.

It was Monday, and the first mail of the day had just come when I knew something was happening to me.

The United States Mail, even though but a handful and most of it addressed to us, is to be treated with respect, not to be trifled with, or kept waiting. Mama, as the assistant postmaster, must attend to the sorting and filling out blanks. Fritz had to carry the mail to a man six miles away, who paid him for this service each day. The babies, fretful with the heat, and no doubt feeling the sadness that pervaded the house, took almost all Mary's time and attention, but there were cooking and household duties to be done too, and the stock had to be cared for, the cows milked.

There we were, three women and four children, all alone, miles from town or neighbors.

It seemed a long time before Mama was free so I could tell her about myself. She was in a daze of sternly repressed grief.

"Oh, honey," Mama implored me, "please don't let anything happen to you now. Anyway, it's not time. You'll just have to wait. There's no one to go for the doctor until Fritz comes home. Anyway," she repeated firmly, "I think you're mistaken; it's not time. Now, you just be quiet and don't let anything happen to you."

That was sensible, reasonable advice. Doctor Miller lived a long distance from us and was the only doctor in the county, thirty-six miles square. This was certainly no time to "let anything happen" to me. I went to my room and lay down.

It was terribly hot. I watched the sand blowing in the hot wind. Finally, I pulled down the window shade and it seemed a little cooler. But I was so uncomfortable, restless and full of strange pains, that I undressed just to have something to do.

Mama came in and sat beside me and patted my hand. Mary looked in every few minutes, smiled encouragingly, and told me not to worry, that I was all right; and hurried back to the little ones or some household task.

Mama came back to tell me that we needed water. We always needed water. She made me promise to remain very quiet, then went out and harnessed the horses to the water wagon in which the water barrels stood. We had to drive several miles to a windmill on a neighbor's ranch. If the wind was blowing, as it usually was, it was not too much of a task to fill the barrels. All one had to do was to drive near enough to hold a bucket beneath the flowing pipe and transfer the water to the barrels. But if the wind was not blowing, the water had to be drawn up hand over hand, bucket by bucket, from an unbelievable depth.

Mama and Fan were gone a long while. When Mama came in, white and breathless, to see how I was feeling, she looked like death. I was terribly ashamed, for in spite of all my efforts, something was definitely happening to me.

Fritz got home at last and Mama hurried him right off again for Doctor Miller. Perhaps from force of habit, he stopped on the way to tell Mrs. McDowell what was happening, and just a little while after my baby made her appearance, with no one in the room to welcome her except a very ignorant mother (Mama had left me alone for a few brief moments), Mrs. McDowell walked in.

I tried to be very quiet and not make any more trouble for anyone. My baby, that I had envisioned as being more beautiful than the angels, was a shocking disappointment. She did not look like a baby at all but like a shrunken and wizened little old man. Like an awful mistake. I knew I was going to love her fiercely to make up for not having made her beautiful, but I could not bear to have my sister, with her lovely babies, or anyone else, look at her. She was premature and very tiny. Fortunately, the hot Texas Maytime took the place of an incubator.

The next day the doctor came, white with weariness. He had had no rest for many hours, having just returned from a far corner of the county where he had battled for the life of another young mother and baby. When told of our need for him, without a moment's rest he rode to our home.

He teased me about my impatience and unwillingness to wait for anything; looked briefly at the baby and told me not to worry about her appearance and size as there was plenty of room in Texas or Nebraska for her to grow, and that she would be taking beauty-prizes in a few months.

He spoke a few words of sympathy to Mama, patted Mrs. McDowell on the shoulder, smoothed back the hair from my forehead and told me to "be good, and mind your elders," went outside, threw his tired leg over his horse, and rode away.

The next day, I was very miserable. I knew Mama and Mary were worried. The baby, I thought, was beginning to look like a baby. But I tumbled and tossed and had strange fancies. That night I thought I was on fire. I could see flames darting and circling above my head. Mama tried to quiet me and keep me in bed. She kept telling me that there was no fire. I could see the fire and became frantic. I reached out to the washstand and

so crowded that there was no room for Mr. Laune. He slept and ate at Mother's. No one had any time to give him any attention. He was lonely, worried, and unhappy. Then, just two weeks after he brought me home, Sister Lucy, Brother Cash's wife, died suddenly. This was a heartbreaking blow for we all loved her. She left four little children, and Mother spent as much of her time as she could with them. Mr. Laune was even more lonely. Even after my nurse was no longer needed and things were running smoothly with Russell and the house, I seemed to have very little time for him.

One mid-afternoon, he came home from the office and asked if I would like to row up the river to a small island where we had often gone soon after we were married. We had a rowboat that we had had a lot of fun with. It was the pride of our hearts, painted white, with red cushions. I had always greeted such jaunts with delight.

When I hesitated, he explained that Mother would oversee the girls with the baby, and he thought I needed to get away from her for a while. I gave elaborate instructions to three experienced women, who looked at me with tolerant amusement. I kissed my child with a yearning that implied a long, long separation.

We took the guitar and a lunch for an early supper and started out on an old-time lark. The river was lovely. Above the old flour mill and dam, the millpond lay still and shiny. The small boat shot out from the bank and the sunlight on the water nearly blinded me, it had been so long since I had been exposed to it. Skimming under the shade cast by the overhanging trees, we rowed past the island to the Point, farther on.

"It's been a long time since we did this," sighed my husband. "Let's sing."

I strummed the accompaniment to his old college songs, the hymns we loved, and the recent popular song, "Sweet Bunch of Daisies." When we reached the Point, we beached the boat, roamed around among the trees, and spread the blankets on the grass and lay side by side looking into the green leaves where birds flitted in and out. We could occasionally hear a fish flop in the water.

It had been a long time since we had been alone to talk, many things had happened to us, and we had much to say to each other.

After a while, we went to hunt mussel shells and then lay on our stomachs on the bank and watched the fish in the clear water. We had a gay supper that reminded us of days soon after we were married. Soon, however, I remarked that we must hurry back home to the baby. "It's time to nurse her," I said, and began to gather things together.

He sat still, his arms around his drawn-up knees. "Not just yet," he said.

The day had died down there among the trees on the point of land jutting out into the river. Darkness lay in the deep shadows along the bank at the east. I wanted to go home. I did not want to sit quietly and talk any longer. Or just sit. And I said so. At first, mildly; then with emphasis.

Mr. Laune did not move.

I held out my hand to pull him to his feet. Instead, he drew me down beside him. "Listen to me," he said, "what do you think you're doing to our marriage?" When I whirled around to see his face he held me to him. "Do you think you're the only woman who ever had a baby? She's mine, too, you must remember; yet you shut me away from her and hardly let me look at her. You're like a selfish little girl with her doll. You won't let anyone else play with it. Why, by golly, you are developing into a stupid-eyed bovine!

"I've been patient until now, because you, have been ill. You've had a ghastly hard experience. But you're never going to get any stronger unless you use your head and stop being a darned maternal idiot. You are letting a few pounds of humanity possess you, consume you, body and soul. You are destroying a living, thinking woman; and I am no longer going to sit idly by and allow it.

"I'm not going to stay at Mother's another night! I'm not going to eat another meal there. We'll rear our child together, like a couple of sensible, adult people, or"—his lips tightened into a straight line—"we'll just snarl and fight it out like a couple of tomcats. I brought you here so we can talk it over, so you can see what you are doing, and decide whether you're going to be a dignified, sensible wife and mother, or an addlepated simpleton. Now, go ahead and say what you want to."

If the Blue River had upended and suddenly spouted skyrockets into the air, I could not have been more astounded and outraged. I had opened my mouth several times during his arraignment, but had closed it like a dying fish, too amazed to make a sound even if he had paused to listen.

But at last I found voice and said what I could think of by way of defense and excuse. I called him some names, too. Nothing I said seemed to reach him. He sat leaning against the tree, his hat pulled low over his eyes, and humming softly to himself.

Once he looked at me and grinned. "You're doing fine," he remarked, "go ahead." He reached into his pocket and pulled out a package, saying casually, "I told Mother we might be late getting back and for her to feed the baby. Is there something else you want to say? Here," he held out the package, "you may need this."

I took it. It was my breast-pump.

In one-tenth of a split second I undid all the centuries of work that my ancestors had accomplished in the way of developing a lady, and descended to the very lowest of cave-woman tactics. I began to cry, and pummel him with my fists. He laughed and caught my hands, holding them tight to protect himself.

"There, there," soothed my husband, when I no longer struggled, "you don't need to live a double life. You just need to use a little understanding, and accept a generally recognized fact that you have a husband, a child, and a home, to love and care for; and in that order, too," he finished firmly. "I have no intention of being put in a corner, sent over to Mother's, or farmed out among the neighbors and friends, simply because we have a baby."

"I thought," I gulped, "that you were more comfortable at Mother's. There was so much confusion at our house, and so little room, I thought you didn't like it."

That was, partially, true. Knowing that he was made comfortable at Mother's left me with a fairly free conscience to give all my time to watching and hovering over the baby.

He patted me and wrung his handkerchief from the river called Blue, and wiped my swollen eyes. "All right now, since you understand that we are the Sidney Laune family, wife and husband, mother and father of a small atom called Russell, and that we are destined to live together—together—" he repeated, "until death us do part. Let's go home."

That fall, Mr. Laune bought a new gun. We hunted everything that flew, crept, ran around on all fours, or climbed trees. All, of course, in season. Mr. Laune had no patience with people who hunted out of season.

We would row up the river for miles, moor the boat near somebody's cornfield where we could hide, lie on our stomachs in the cold damp, and wait for a lot of pretty ducks to assemble on the water. Then, for some reason that I never understood, for we did not hunt with decoys, the ducks would be impelled to whirr into the air, and we would shoot.

I mean Mr. Laune would shoot. Everything that makes a hunter was left out of my composition. I simply served as audience. I didn't have a gun, and wouldn't have aimed it at anything and pulled the trigger if I had had one.

I kept my eyes shut and winced when the gun went off, then I would jump up and squeal in admiration—though I wanted to weep—if I saw a pitiful bunch of feathers hurtle to the ground or plummet into the water. And I learned to say in the correct tone of disappointment—while secretly rejoicing—"O-o-h, you missed," when a lovely whole duck went winging to a safer place.

One cold, cloudy day we rowed up the river as usual. The low hillsides were crackling with hoarfrost, and the cornstalks that littered the fields were slippery. I was wearing Mr. Laune's long stiff yellow slicker over my coat, and running, slipping rather, along behind him, trying to heed his command, "Quiet!" as well as I could; when suddenly, my feet shot out from under me and I sat down. Hard.

I had gone down with such emphasis that my head was spinning. When I tried to scramble to my feet, a wave of nausea swept over me. Mr. Laune gave me a wide sweeping motion of his hand that I hoped meant, "Keep quiet and stay where you are."

I never obeyed a command more thankfully. Pretty soon, I heard his loud whisper: "C'mon, don't stay there all day; they're gathering in the cove by the hundreds. It's about three hundred feet further. C'mon."

I tried to smile brightly and companionably, "You just go on," I said, "I'll stay here."

He came striding back and knelt down beside me. "What are you doing down there? Get up! The ducks! Hundreds of them, I tell you! What's the matter with you?" An anxious fretful tone came into his voice whenever anything menaced his family. "Tired?"

"I slipped," I explained. "I'm all right. You go on. I think— I think—"

"Are you hurt?"

"I think—I broke—my neck."

He twisted my neck experimentally. "No, you haven't," he said, relieved.

"Or—my back. Or—maybe my legs." He and the cornstalks were floating around in a crazy mist. He nearly pulled my legs out of their sockets, keeping an anxious eye on the cove that was filling fast with ducks.

"There's nothing the matter with your legs," he said. "Get up and come on."

"You go on," I urged, "I think I hurt my arm, maybe." I tried to tuck my right arm out of his way.

There was a chattering and murmuring among the ducks, and his eyes brightened. "Here," he said briskly, "you're all right; right as a trivet. Come on."

I started to snuggle down again. "You get them, I'll wait here."

"No, by golly! I want you to see them!"

It was no use arguing any longer. I gave him my left hand

and struggled to my feet. My right hand, with its red mitten that Father had knit, dangled curiously. I tried to pick it up with my left hand and turned. "I'm going home," I announced stubbornly.

He held me back. "You can't do that. Honey, what's the matter?"

"I'm sorry," I replied, "but I'm sure my right arm is broken." I backed away from him so he wouldn't investigate, and showed him my hand falling backward.

With a leap, he started to pick me up in his arms. He had tossed his gun aside.

Carrying me was so absurd that I laughed. "Pick up your gun, we can't lose that. And I can walk, there's nothing the matter with my legs." With the nausea gone, I felt quite able to walk.

Fritz, who had come to us in time to start school in September, met us at the door with Russell draped over his hip. He was the best nurse anyone could want. But there was the house to be kept (Ida, the girl who helped me, was in Lincoln having an ulcerated tooth treated), meals to be cooked, and the baby to be cared for when he was in school; and as my right arm was soon in a huge cast, Mr. Laune sent for Mama. I think he had been wanting an excuse to have her come, anyway. Now, he had it.

How we got along the week before she arrived from Little Rock, only the angels know; but we managed, and even had a lot of fun in a slipshod sort of way. Of course, after she came, and Ida, my excellent helper, got back from Lincoln, life moved along like a song.

Mr. Laune asked one day, "Mama, did you ever read *Uncle Tom's Cabin?*"

Mama replied in her gentle voice, "No, Sidney, I never did; but I've heard about it."

"Did you?" he turned to me.

"No, it wasn't a popular novel at home; but I know who wrote it."

He grinned, and said nothing more.

That evening, we three walked down to the post office to get the mail. We often stopped off at one of the neighbors, or strolled up to Mother's after getting the mail, so I was not suspicious when Mr. Laune told Ida that we might be late coming home.

There was a shabby circus-tent on lower Main Street, with huge posters announcing that "A Dramatic and Spectacular" performance of *Uncle Tom's Cabin* was to be given in the tent that night.

Mr. Laune herded Mama and me over near the entrance on which almost everyone in town was converging. "Let's go in and see it," he urged excitedly, just as though he did not have three tickets to the show already in his pocket, and was not pushing us before him through the entrance.

Inside, there were tiers of seats and Mr. Laune led us to them while an usher explained, "No reserved seats, Mister. One's as good as another. Take your choice, and step right up, ladies, step right up."

"Perhaps we'd better get to the top," suggested Mr. Laune, "so no one will knock against your arm."

We climbed to the top layer. Friends came in and called to us, and we settled ourselves to watch the crowd gather. As an usher dashed up and down the steps escorting people to their places, I felt the seats quiver. "There's no danger of this thing falling down, is there?" I asked.

"No danger at all, Miss. Perfectly safe. Step right up, folks."

There was a lot of stepping. The kerosene lamps swung and smoked and smelled. The play began.

Uncle Tom, with the most original accent I ever heard, soliloquized while he tried to keep his gray, motheaten wig and whiskers in place. Simon Legree cracked his whip around his shiny new boots, and Little Eva danced in and knelt beside Uncle Tom and looked coyly into his face.

Everything was going nicely, when there was a warning creak, and the seats swayed gently. Then, with a tired sigh, they started to lie down, hesitated, decided not to dillydally about it and flopped to the ground.

Pandemonium broke loose. The lights, turned low to add to the illusion of the play, were lost in a haze of dust. Women and children screamed and cried. Men shouted and swore. The manager and his helpers yelled at everyone to be quiet.

My skirts were caught under the seat and I couldn't rise. I humped forward over my cast and tried to keep the surging mob from stepping on me. I could hear Mr. Laune calling me, but it was impossible to make him hear my answers. Doctors were called for. The injured moaned, and others wept. Everyone screamed directions to everyone else and no one paid any attention.

I thought as I sat there with my head between my knees, and folks milling around and over me, how disappointed Mr. Laune would be to have his little party spoiled in this ghastly way. Then I felt my shoulder grasped, and heard him mutter. "My lord, are you all in one piece, or have they stamped you to a pulp?" When I grinned up at him, he stooped down and hugged me fiercely. "Are you hurt? What do you mean by sitting there in the dirt?" He released my skirts and lifted me to my feet.

By that time we were almost the only ones left in the tent. The manager was begging tearfully, "Come back tomorrow, folks, and you'll be admitted free. Give us a chance. You'll see the most spectacular—"

Mama, who had been pushed along by the crowd, came up to us smoothing her skirt and straightening her hat. "I have always heard that *Uncle Tom's Cabin* upsets people from the South, but I didn't dream that Nonie and I would have such a complete collapse. What are we going to do now, Sidney?"

"We're going to see *Uncle Tom's Cabin*. That's what we came for, isn't it?" he replied, with set teeth. "You both stay right here. I'll be back."

He motioned to the manager, and they went out of the tent, returning in a little while with three packing boxes they had taken from Brother Cash's store. They placed these on the ground in front of the stage.

"Sit down," Mr. Laune commanded Mama and me. We sat

down. "Now," he turned to the manager, who was wringing his hands beside us, "put on your show." And he sat down on his box.

A few other people straggled in, and seeing us, went out and got some sort of seats, and we saw a complete performance of *Uncle Tom's Cabin*.

Of course, we shouldn't have been sitting almost on the ground where we could see the underpinnings of the blocks of ice over which Eliza, with little yips and squeaks of fright gamboled like a mountain goat. The "ravening bloodhounds" we had been promised must have been tamed considerably by the recent unhappy turmoil, for they hopped languidly, with sad-eyed persistence, from one tipsy block to another, until one sat down on the ice and began an energetic scratching. The block did a spirited cadenza, and his companion in the chase, reminded of *his* fleas, sat down on another block.

That was when Mr. Laune, who had been sitting with his arms folded across his chest, and his lips tightened grimly, began to enjoy the show. He threw back his head and gave a joyous shout.

When Little Eva, after a sad farewell, began her ascent into Heaven, the wires by which she was being assisted aloft, stuck. There she hung, between heaven and earth, her long nightgown blowing in the breeze, revealing her black-stockinged legs striking out wildly, while the men behind the scenes could be heard swearing and cursing.

That act brought applause, loud and sustained. Mr. Laune almost blistered his palms, while I tapped smartly on my nice hard cast.

As we were going home, Mama said in her soft, serious voice, "You know, Sidney, *Uncle Tom's Cabin* was just about what I expected. Thank you for taking us."

Mr. Laune glanced at her obliquely, and the corners of his mouth twitched as he said, politely, "You're welcome, Mama."

6 *Musical Comedy War*

When I was a little child, our gardener had rheumatism, our cook had a bone-felon, and I was fed stories of the War Between the States. All these miseries—rheumatism, bone-felon, and war—made a deep impression on my mind, and I had agonized in the first real prayer I ever prayed that I might be spared the affliction of all three.

Up to this time, my prayer had been answered.

When war with Spain became imminent, Captain Culver—I think he had a higher rank at this time—wanted Mr. Laune to go with his cavalry unit of the National Guard.

With typical male finesse, Mr. Laune put the matter up to me. "What do you think about it? Do you think I should go? Can you get along without me?"

I knew exactly what I thought about it. We had a baby not a year old, and I knew as much about business as a blind kitten. But I also knew how much he wanted to join Captain Culver; and I did so hate to have him denied anything he wanted. He asked for so little for himself. So I used a little feminine finesse.

"I think you should do what you think best. I believe I could manage the store"—he had bought an implement store next door to the office—"if you can teach me."

Then, feeling like Delilah, I waited anxiously to see what he would do.

War against Spain was declared April 25, 1898, though a state of war had virtually existed since the twenty-first. Mr. Laune was unhappy and secretly rebellious about staying at home. When he was about eighteen years old, Captain Culver had seen in him the makings of a fine lieutenant and troop leader and the very young Mr. Laune had thrown himself into this work with enthusiasm; more enthusiasm, his father had thought unsympathetically, than he displayed in the work of the office.

Soon it had become evident that the youthful troop leader should be mounted on an animal suitable to his position, and Captain Culver had found a horse that he had thought met all requirements. Mr. Laune declared that the animal must have been seventeen hands high, with long legs disproportionate to the rest of him. Nevertheless, he and Captain Culver regarded it as their idea of a charger, and were proud of its impressive size.

A big review had been scheduled to be held in Lincoln, the capital, and the newly organized Cavalry Troop A was to participate for the first time. The heterogeneous group had been so busy with their regular work that it had been difficult for them to get together for any serious drilling. However, the farmhands, cowboys, and townsmen who had joined up—furnishing their own mounts, of course—were looking forward to their big day when they would be reviewed by the Governor.

When the festive day arrived, Lincoln was crowded. People had come from miles around to enjoy a carnival holiday, to hear the speeches, and to see the militia parade. It had been decided that Troop A, though small in number and mostly devoid of uniforms and military trappings, was to get its share of attention by making a lively demonstration. The plan was for it to line up on one side of the field, then, when a small cannon was fired, the troop was to charge across the field past the review stand.

Sitting on the tallest horse in the outfit—possibly the tallest horse in the state—Mr. Laune had taken his station alongside the cannon and in his most military manner had ordered his men to form a straight line, and to conduct themselves with the precision of seasoned cavalrymen. The Captain signaled with his saber. The cannon went off with an earthshaking *Bang*.

After one spasmodic leap and convulsive shudder, Mr. Laune's horse folded his long legs beneath him and collapsed in a dead faint. The Captain was indeed dashing in front of the reviewing stand, followed by a few of his troopers going in the same general direction, but some troopers were lying on the ground, others seemed to be playing a confused game of leap-frog, while the spectators were scrambling wildly out of the uncertain path of the runaway horses. . . .

In spite of, or perhaps because of this debacle—in which no one, miraculously, was hurt—Mr. Laune still yearned for military glory.

One day, before war with Spain was actually declared, Captain Culver and one of his lieutenants came to see me. I thought they were going to urge me to be big-hearted, and with flags flying and a patriotic wave of my hand, send my husband off to war. But after a few minutes they gave me the real reason for their call.

They wanted Dexter, the horse Brother Cash had given me for my wedding gift.

It is true I was not riding Dexter at that time, because of my broken arm, the baby, and increased household duties. But Mr. Laune had broken him to harness, and he served proficiently and decoratively between the shafts of my swanky buggy. I could not bear the thought of giving him up. He was so gentle and intelligent; and such a gentleman about his intelligence, never making me feel conscious of my stupidity when he thought it best to take matters in his own hooves or bit.

I explained to the two uniformed gentlemen why I could not sell my horse to the Army. "He was a wedding gift," I gulped.

"Yes, I know," replied Captain—or Major, or maybe Colonel, by this time—Culver, carelessly.

"And he's so well trained," I went on. "For us, I mean. I need him. I can't get along without him." I didn't like the patronizing air of these two military men. They looked so elegantly polished, and they had caught me looking frowzy and untidy. No woman in that condition can argue with a well-groomed man with any sort of dignity, so I said, flatly and firmly, "And I'm not going to sell him."

I had always liked Captain Culver, too, but that was when he was just a genial neighbor and good friend, before he wanted to take my husband and horse to war with him.

When Mr. Laune came home, he "reasoned" with me. He pointed out that there were many distasteful things we must do when our country is at war. "If I can't go, and it does seem as if that's impossible," he looked at me accusingly, "you can at least be patriotic enough to let Dexter go."

That made me ashamed. But I was getting pretty tired, I told him, of having to compromise every question by doing what somebody else wanted me to do. "Anyway," I said stubbornly, "I'm not going to let Dexter go."

But of course I did. I was afraid to push matters too far, for the spectacular demonstrations of war, with speeches, and parades, uniforms and flags, and things like that, were getting more and more dramatic. I didn't know how long Mr. Laune could stand on the sidelines, or when he would find his patriotism overcoming his domestic responsibilities. I was afraid he might jump into a uniform, snatch a flag, and ride away singing about the girl he left behind him.

So one sad day, the boys went marching away with Dexter, ridden by the handsome lieutenant, somewhere near the head of the column. I watched him through a fog of tears, praying that they all might soon be coming back again.

He did not come back. Neither did the handsome young lieutenant, whom he bore so proudly.

By the time word came of battles in which our men were dying and suffering, there was no place in my consciousness for petty selfishness about Dexter. I have heard it said that that was "a musical comedy war," but to those who lost their sons and husbands it was real enough.

Then, in a little while, the war was over, and we could enjoy our happiness without any feeling of guilt. We were all so busy that I was a little slow in realizing the significance of a stomach upheaval that grew steadily more pronounced.

A neighbor, whose small daughter was about Russell's age, came in our back door one morning while I was occupied in the bathroom. When I came out, white and shaken, and leaned against the sink in the kitchen, she eyed me solemnly.

"Forgoshalmitysakesalive," she intoned in shocked surprise, "you don't mean to tell me!"

I hadn't meant to tell her anything, but I nodded sickishly.

"Well! I call it a darned shame. A darned, lowdown shame. I call it a insult. A darned insult. And let me tell you something," she went on, her hands on her hips, "if my husband ever expects me to have another baby, I'll be—I'll be—insulted!"

It was the first time I had ever heard the matter expressed quite that way.

Not too many weeks later Mr. Laune came into the house from the barn and said with a grin, "Well, what do you know? Myrt's been insulted." We had already incorporated that word into our special vocabulary.

"How do you know?" I asked, with a shameless feeling of satisfaction.

"She was out in their back yard hanging onto the fence, proclaiming it to the world."

It was a long winter. Mr. Laune bought a new team and surrey. When spring came we all took long rides in the country,
and walks along the river. I was possessed to dig in the garden
and plant flowers in our new yard. The wait grew tiresome.

Mama and I were sewing one day while Mr. Laune, with Russell in his lap, read aloud to us. He laid the book aside and sat
for a moment quietly staring into space. Then, he asked:

"Mama, would it be a—a—disgrace, if this baby should be another girl?"

"No, Sidney, I don't think so," Mama replied, placidly.

For a moment, I was too astonished at his question to speak.
I knew he wanted desperately for the baby to be a boy, but,
"Indeed," I snapped, "I wouldn't be disgraced to have another
sweet little girl like Russell."

He sat up horrified. His devotion to Russell was the joke of
the town. He caught her closer in his arms. "We couldn't have
another one like her," he said. "She was dropped into our life by
—a gracious Providence. It couldn't happen again. We don't
deserve it."

Our son was born that night. His father was beside himself
with joy. Before nine o'clock the next morning, he was holding
a reception in the dining room, showing Paul Sidney to his
friends.

It was May again, and a day or two after the baby came, Mr.
Laune came into our bedroom and threw the shades to the top of
the windows. Then, without a word, he began to pull and haul
my bed across the room until it lay alongside the double windows,
while the nurse, Mama, and I kept up a chorus, "What are you
doing? What is the matter?"

Twisting my head around, I could see, in full bloom, framed
by the window, the crab apple tree. It seemed that not one more
blossom could have found space on the widespread branches.
The perfume floated into the open windows.

Both our babies had come in May, their birthdays five days
apart, and we planned always to have a crab apple tree in bloom
at this time every year. Of course, we never had another, but

the lack was supplied to me by a bottle of perfume tucked beneath my pillow when those May days came around, each year afterward.

Though clumsy and inept with his hands, Mr. Laune was sure he could do anything that was needed for his son. Paul was only a few weeks old when his father came home from the office one evening, evidently depressed. I knew that something had disturbed him, but I waited until we were alone and the lights out before asking him the reason.

"Why did you let me go to the office with those darned safety pins decorating my coat?" he burst out.

"Did you do that?" I asked, smiling in the dark.

"Of course I did," he snapped, "and not a soul had the decency to say a word. I went all over town—to the bank, to the mill, and in all the stores. I know now the reason everyone grinned, and seemed so jovial. But do you think that anyone, Cash, or Van, or anyone, had the decency to tell me that those three shining safety pins were spread across my coat?"

Now that his father's estate had been settled, Mr. Laune was free to leave Milford and our first plan was to move to Omaha City where some college friends of his wanted him to settle. We had in fact gone so far as to select a house and I was all set to enjoy the delights of a real city. Before that move could be made, however, he had to cut his business ties in Woodward, and a short while before Christmas he went off to Oklahoma.

He had been gone about ten days when I received a letter asking if I would be willing to return to Woodward for about five years, when the question of school for the children would arise.

I stuck to my usual formula, "Whatever you think best, is all right with me."

That is a form of dishonesty that now makes me blush. It gives a woman a virtuous feeling, permits her to slide out of all responsibility, and later, if things don't work out satisfactorily, she can throw all the blame on her husband.

Mr. Laune must have pushed the train all the way back to

Nebraska after receiving my letter; and never was there such frenzied dismantling of a home and packing of furniture and household goods. He sent me and the babies to stay with Mama, who had bought a house around the corner from ours, during the process of ripping up carpets, tearing down curtains and pictures, throwing all the loose things in boxes and barrels and chucking them into a boxcar, and shipping the whole wild mess to Woodward.

Two weeks after I sent my letter expressing willingness to go to Oklahoma, we were on the train.

I am so constructed that after I have run gaily across a bridge and recklessly burned it behind me, I want to be back on the safe side of the comfort of old ways and places. I thought with acute longing of the pretty homes in Omaha. I thought of the noble trees, the green grassy lawns, the electric lights, plumbing, gas, and all the comforts and gracious living, none of which we would have in Oklahoma. Now I was committed to parched grass, if any; to kerosene lamps with smoky chimneys and charred wicks; to a perpetual lack of water, and coal or oil stoves that kept everything black with soot; to endless wind and sand.

Well, the decision was made, and here we were, January 1, 1900, racing back to all these discomforts. And while I told myself that I could not bear the trials I knew were before me, my heart lifted to meet them. I suspected there was something wrong with the inside of my head, and I grinned to myself as I imagined how bitterly I was going to complain, and how, in my heart, I would love being back in my beloved Southwest.

7 Woodward, Oklahoma Territory

The Central Hotel in Woodward was full. Judge Dean, who had met us at the train, told the hack driver to take us to his home. His family had come to him soon after we were married, and they had built a large house on the site where he had driven his stake that first day of the Opening. It made no difference that their home was full of their own children and grandchildren;

Judge and Mrs. Dean gathered the four of us into it, and into
their hearts, along with the others.

We stayed there a week, until our furniture came and we
moved into the only place we could find, a small house across the
tracks near the roundhouse and railroad shops, a long way from
town. We unpacked only such things as we needed for immediate use, because we hoped to get a more desirable place in which
to live permanently.

Mr. Laune was plunged immediately into work at the office
and had no time to remember that he had a family; much less,
time to do anything for us. The grocery stores made delivery of
orders but they had to be given personally, as there were no
telephones then. If I wanted a loaf of bread, or anything at all
from the store, all I had to do was to chop the frozen water from
the barrel in the yard, heat it on the coal stove, bathe and dress
the two babies, park them in the middle of the bed while I
dressed, bank the fire in the stove, wrap the babies in their coats
and blankets, put them in the buggy, and sally forth in the wind
and sand.

Mr. Laune always teased me about the baby-buggy. I had been
determined to have the handsomest carriage in the state of Nebraska for Russell. Not one in Milford would do. Our merchants
furnished catalogues and offered to order whatever we selected.
But I thought nothing we saw was fine enough. Consequently,
we carried the baby in our arms for the first few months. Then
one day, when I started downtown with her, a neighbor suggested that I put her in the carriage her child had outgrown a
number of years before. It was in the garret but she dragged it
down, brushed off the dust, and I piled my blankets, pillows and
baby in it. It proved quite satisfactory—pending the time we
could find the carriage of my dreams.

And you know very well what happened. After I had used it
for a few weeks, we paid five dollars for it and I forgot about the
magnificent one I had wanted. When Paul came, it seemed foolish to bother about getting another, so we continued to use the
old carriage for both children. It was large and roomy, and had a

long Main Street. The small one-storey buildings had high "false fronts" from which covered porches protruded. As the buildings were often separated by vacant lots, the porch floors did not form a continuous walk but had steps at either end. Negotiating these steps with a baby carriage and two babies required both strength and skill.

Bordering both sides of the street, a few feet away from the broken walk, there were hitching rails made of sturdy posts joined by two rough, heavy, boards. To this rail were tied teams hitched to wagons and buggies. The cowboys' ponies, bearing heavy saddles, stood near the rack with reins swinging loose. During the winter months they would often stand all day humped in tight knots of misery against the wind and sleet and snow. In the hot summer they would drowse in the sunshine, flicking flies with languid tails and twitching their ears.

Fashionably dressed young mothers paraded the streets holding up their trailing skirts as they pushed their baby-buggies through the sand, and up and down the little steps between the stores. Those who were brave, or not strong enough to manage the steps, risked the trail between the hitching rack and the porches; sometimes an acquisitive horse reached out a long pointed nose to nibble at the flowers on a passing hat, or a shaggy bronc would scare a young mother half out of her life by shying at the buggy and rearing on his hind legs.

I don't know how on earth we held up our long skirts, pushed a baby-buggy, managed a lace parasol, and buffeted the wind, all at the same time. But we did, because we had to. It was stylish to wear long skirts and carry a parasol. Maybe it was stylish to have babies, too; certainly we had them. I don't know about the wind. I suppose that was thrown in for good measure; that, and the sand.

We were very crowded and uncomfortable in the little house, even though much of our furniture was still in crates. But houses were scarce, and I was hard to please. I was not at all interested in the places Mr. Laune presented for my approval. They were too cramped in a town where there was all the room in the world. I wanted a large yard, not too near other houses, where my children could play. The prolonged search required a team and buggy.

When we went to Nebraska, Harboldt and Broncho had been left with Judge Dean, their co-owner with Mr. Laune, so we bought two horses from Mr. Champion, the liveryman. Mr. Champion was a fine, low-voiced old man who had raised Flora and Fauna from colts. When I expressed my surprise at the names he had given them, he told me slyly that he always chose names for his horses "for a reason." I never did discover that particular reason, but they were a good, gentle team.

Every chance we had we drove around the town, which was scattered over a good deal of land, looking for a place to buy. On one such trip, Mr. Laune pointed with the whip at a small dwelling of four rooms—two in front, and two shed-rooms at the rear—and remarked that a railroad engineer who lived there had recently been transferred to Wellington, Kansas.

"Then the house will be empty. Do you suppose we could buy it?" I asked.

"We couldn't live there. It's in the wrong part of town. John Buswell is on the Santa Fe, and this is convenient to his work. It's too near the railroad for us, and too near the red-light district."

I had never heard of a red-light district, and I thought he referred to the red and green warning lights along the track. "I wouldn't mind that. We could fence that big yard for the babies. Please, let's see about it."

He argued, and explained about the "district."

"But a lot of nice people live in this neighborhood, too."

"Yes, of course. The engineer who lives in this house, and the one over on that corner; but they live here because it's convenient for them. And the Reynolds, who live on the hill, homesteaded their place. But this is a poor place to buy."

I continued to coax. That was where I wanted to live. The "district" to which he referred was about four blocks away, and at last he yielded, with reluctance, to the extent that he agreed we might look at it.

The interior of the plain small house was a surprise. Mrs. Buswell was a genius at making four little rooms seem twice that many, as well as attractive and homelike. Actually, it was exactly like most other Woodward houses, no bigger, no smaller, no worse, no better.

After a few days we did buy the place, in spite of Mr. Laune's warning:

"You won't like it here."

It was now March, and Court was in session. Mr. Laune had no time to help me uncrate and unpack the furniture, and there was no other help available. I worked like a mad thing early and late. The babies had to get along on the fringe of time.

One morning while I was nursing the baby, and was taking this time to tell Russell a story as she leaned against my shoulder, she gave a sudden cry, and blood spurted from her nose.

"What happened?" I cried.

"I put the hook-shoe in my nose and I can't get it out," she answered with a frightened whimper.

"You did what?"

"The hook-shoe, from your dress. I put it in my nose," she repeated, while I tried to check the flow.

She always transposed compound words; knob-door, bread-corn, pin-hair, hook-shoe. But there was no shoe-hook near my dress.

"Show me." The blood was streaming down, and she was so little and so frightened. I looked around for the shoe-hook that I used to button our shoes; but she showed me where a hook-and-eye had come loose from my dress. Apparently, absorbed by the story, she had absent-mindedly poked it up her nose. I tried to reach it, but she was bleeding so severely that I dared not make further attempts. There was no one to send for a doctor, and no telephone.

I could not wait to change my dress, or even my house slippers —red satin things with fur around the tops. I had to get her to a doctor, and I did not know one in the town. I bundled the two children into their buggy and raced down the road, over the tracks, and on to the town.

"Hold the handkerchief to your nose and breathe through your mouth." Of course she had been taught never to breathe through her mouth. "Don't cry. You're all right. The doctor will take it out in just a minute. Don't touch it; just keep very quiet. Don't be frightened. Mama's not frightened a bit, because the doctor knows just how to take it out."

Bareheaded, I ran like a crazy thing down the long Main Street until I saw the sign of a doctor's office. J. M. Workman, Physician and Surgeon. I had never laid eyes on him.

I talked to Russell every step of the way. Running and talking, I tore into the doctor's office and, suddenly, I could not speak a word. I simply handed him my child, and slumped into a chair somebody pushed under me.

In no time at all, he removed the thing, bathed Russell's face and applied a soothing ointment. Then came the journey home—in a rumpled house dress covered with blood, sloppy red satin slippers, hair flying, and everyone, I thought, staring at me. It was a nightmare; but inside of me I kept a prayer of thanksgiving singing in my heart. My little girl was all right, and had not been hurt too cruelly; and I knew that she would never again put anything up her nose.

Then, a few days later, the baby was taken alarmingly sick. On his way to the courthouse where he asked the Judge to excuse him from the morning session, Mr. Laune stopped at Doctor Patton's office and begged him to hurry to the house.

After examining the baby the doctor prescribed some medicine from his bag of remedies, and turned to me.

"There's nothing the matter with this fellow that a nice long rest for the mother won't cure. You're so tired that your milk is an active poison to this little one. Better stop nursing him. But more important, stop being a dray horse and just be a mother." He patted my shoulder, while I nodded meekly.

The day after Doctor Patton's visit, Mr. Laune came home

with a Negro man in tow whose name was Frank. Frank was a former soldier who, when troops were transferred from Fort Supply, elected to remain near the old post and filed on land in the county. Mr. Laune left Frank with me and hurried back to the office.

"I purely didn't want to come here," he complained to me aggrievedly as he watched Mr. Laune go swinging back to town, "but dat man, he's de most commandinest man, and he wouldn' lissen to no reason. So, here I is."

Even though he didn't want to do it, Frank did a good day's work, beating and laying carpets, and unpacking and moving furniture. In the late afternoon, I asked him how much I owed him.

He drew himself up haughtily, and informed me with great dignity that he didn't "take no pay from no lady."

"I'll talk to de boss-man about wages," he said, "he's de one what hired me." Then, with a chuckle, he relieved my hurt feelings by adding, "Besides, lawdy, Missy, you don't owe me nothin', you's jes my kind."

He bowed and swept the ground with a flourish of his battered old soldier's hat as he paid me this compliment, then climbed aboard his motheaten horse and rode away.

Later, Mr. Laune said to me with a smile, "I wish, if you can ever induce Frank to work for you again that you'd manage somehow, without insulting his dignity, to pay him. I've paid him for that day's work several times; but every time he comes to town he hunts me up and reminds me, 'Say, Boss, dat sho is a mighty fine little wife you got. 'Member, dat time I worked so hard all dat long day to he'p her? 'Member how much I he'p her? Say Boss, I's mighty dry ridin' in from my farm.'"

I don't think the debt I owed Frank for that day's work was ever cancelled until his death, many years later.

As I went on trying to be a mother instead of a "dray horse," the housework suffered while I played and read to the children, until Mr. Laune came home bringing with him a pretty girl.

"This is Kitty," he told me. "She's going to help you with the work for a while."

Kitty smiled shyly and started in to make friends with the children and straighten up the house. That night, Mr. Laune told me that she was from the red-light district, and involved in some sort of difficulty that had to be settled by court action. A man visiting the district had been robbed of his money.

"He had no business visiting the district, did he?" I asked. "And anyway, if he went there he ought to have been robbed. I don't believe Kitty had anything to do with it. I think she's a nice, sweet girl."

"Well, of course," Mr. Laune replied judiciously, "there is a difference of opinion regarding the district; there are some who contend that it's a business, and should be run on respectable and honest lines." He grinned at me. "However, we won't go into that. I want Kitty to help you, and have had her paroled to me pending trial."

Kitty was the joy of my life. She was strong, quiet, willing, and industrious. She had a delicious wit, a low, sweet voice, and when she laughed, as she did readily and joyously, the babies came running, laughing with her. She had what is known as "the true mother touch," and they adored her.

Often her work was interrupted by the sheriff, or one of his deputies, coming to take her to the courthouse for more questioning. She would return to us pale and tired, and sit quietly with the children in her lap. I asked no questions.

As soon as the case in court was settled, and Kitty was free, she left our home and our town, to my sorrow.

One of the first things we did after purchasing our property was to plant an orchard of peach trees. Then one day the station-agent told Mr. Laune about a shipment of black locust trees that for some reason had not been accepted by the consignee, and were lying in the freight office.

"How many are there?"

"Several thousand."

"Can they be bought?"

"Yes, and cheap."

spring water from his claim several miles south of town, and filled our two barrels that stood along the edge of our yard.

In the summertime, wiggletails flirted merrily in the barrels that stood in the blazing sun. We boiled and strained the drinking water, poured it into jars that were wrapped in wet cloths and placed them in a draft of air to cool. We merely strained the bath water. No heating was necessary; the sun took care of that. But in winter Spartan courage and endurance were required to chop the ice out of the barrels.

Trees were Mr. Laune's primary project, but it seemed to me that a cistern was the first consideration. So Jake Eckert began to dig us a cistern, and we had the house fitted with gutters in anticipation of the time when the cistern would be completed and the rains would fall.

Mr. Buswell had left behind him, besides the flock of game-chickens, Jack and Daisy, a loft of beautiful pigeons. The pigeons —fantails, pouters, and other varieties—were the most decorative things that ever cooed sweetly and engagingly on a roof. They sat in a long irridescent row on the ridgepole and while the pouters pouted and the fantails spread their tails, they stepped in a pink-toed, measured minuet. They thought the new gutters had been supplied for their special benefit.

At long last the cistern was completed. There was a bright new filter with charcoal and screening, and an ingenious pump with a long chain fitted with little cups was ready to draw up the water when it came through the long lines of gutters and pipes and flowed into the filter and down into the cistern.

And then it rained! We watched water sluice into the filter, and after the rain, we rushed out to see water, our very own water, and to pump it up with those cute little cups on the chain.

But Mr. Laune discovered that birds' nests, eggs, tiny pink naked baby sparrows, as well as generous contributions from the pigeons and a goodly portion of Oklahoma sand had washed into the filter and screen. . . . So the cistern had to be emptied and scrubbed and new charcoal bought for the filter. I nearly wept to see all that water wasted, that we had prayed for so long.

Thereafter, it became a race between me and the sparrows to keep the gutters free from filth, nests, sticks and baby sparrows. As fast as the boys I hired could claw out the trash, the birds patiently filled them again. The ancient urge to build and produce was not affected by my efforts at cleanliness. Nor could I do anything about the pigeons who continued to march in regal splendor along the gutters and ridgepole.

However, the little switch that turned the water from the filter took care of their careless, unsanitary habits—if I thought of it in time. If a cloud no larger than a man's hand appeared in the sky in the northwest, I dashed out to see that the gadget was turned to the ground so that the gutters would be sluiced clean. Turning it back to the filter while an Oklahoma deluge soaked me to the skin was something to be grimly endured; every drop had to be conserved, for rains were few and far between.

When I became too discouraged, I would long for the flesh-pots of Egypt. Then I would remind Mr. Laune of the five year plan, and urge wistfully, "Let's go back to Omaha." (Or Kansas City, Denver, Wichita, anywhere where there was water, gas, telephones, and domestic help.)

He would look at me in puzzled astonishment. "What for? What would we *do* there? Why honey, we're helping to *build* this place. It's a fine place to live, and will be better. Those places are all *made*. I don't want to live any place where I can't fight for my way."

A few days after one of these conversations, Mr. Laune came home standing on top of the dray and clutching a tall piece of furniture in his arms. At his shout for me I rushed to lend assistance, admiration, sympathy, or whatever the occasion seemed to demand.

He was brimming over with pleasure. I hated to blurt out the question: "Whatever is that thing?"

"That thing" was a golden oak cabinet, or closet, about seven or eight feet tall. Mr. Laune and the drayman brought it into the house and put it in the living room, where Mr. Laune stood holding it up, looking around for some more suitable place. There simply wasn't any. He relinquished his grip cautiously and paid the driver who went away.

"What's it for? What's inside it?" I finally asked as he went charging around the four rooms that were already packed to their full capacity.

He looked at me fretfully. "Where do you want it?" he asked.

"Want it?" I snapped back. "I don't even know what the thing is."

"It's a bathtub. Where do you want it?"

Well, certainly, we needed a bathtub more than the king of the cannibal islands needed religion, and I should have fallen upon it with loud cries of joy, but in our crowded house I could see no place for it, unless we stood it cheek by jowl with the piano. There we could take a bath almost publicly.

"This is the way it works." His enthusiasm returning, he released some sort of fastening, and with a little straining and pulling, the tall cabinet lowered itself to the floor, revealing a shiny tin tub, the very longest tub I had ever seen. Long and narrow, like Barbara Allen's grave.

> "Oh Mother dear, make down my bed,
> And make it long and narrow,"

I sang feelingly.

"There you go," he said, deeply hurt. "You howl for months on end for a bathtub, and when I go to the trouble to find you one, look at you."

I looked at me, and at his happiness that I had dimmed.

"What's that machinery?" I asked brightly.

"Oh, that?" It took such a little encouragement to have him radiant again. "Well, you see, the top tank is for water. You fill it and light this gasoline burner here beneath it, and it heats the water. See? And this tank is for gasoline. Pretty slick, isn't it?"

I thought his enthusiasm was running away with him when he added, "I'll fill the water tank every morning before I go to the office, and all you'll have to do is to light the burner."

"That will be wonderful," I told him admiringly.

And it was pretty slick when you remembered the washtub hanging on a nail on the outside of the kitchen, and banging away in the wind. All you had to do with *that*, was bring it into the house, set it in the middle of the floor, and fill it, bucket by bucket, from the barrel at the edge of the street, reversing the process when your bath was over.

"See if you can close it."

I grunted and lifted the thing to position so it hid the insides. And there it stood, like the leaning tower of Pisa, in the middle of our living-room floor, and there as far as I could see, it would have to remain.

"Where did you get it?" I asked. I should have known; I did know. From Brockhaus, where we, and everyone else, got everything.

"From Brockhaus," he echoed my thought. "It came from Fort Supply when the post was abandoned. Belonged to an Army officer there."

"What a man," I murmured, letting my eyes travel from the bottom to the top of the cabinet.

"There you go again," he sighed, despairingly. "Can't you appreciate anything? This is a good tub. Not a flaw in it; not a scratch on the cabinet. And there's room enough for me to stretch my legs. I'm pretty darned tired, if you ask me, of curling up like a grubworm every time I take a bath."

"I know," I agreed quickly. "All I want to know is, where are we going to put it. It can't stay here, can it?"

He made another survey of the house and came back with a defeated air to where I was holding up the leaning tower, rubbed his brow, and looked troubled. "No place," he admitted. Then, like sunlight over cloudy water, his face lightened, he snatched at his hat.

"Where are you going?" I bleated after him.

He paused in his flight through the doorway. "I just thought of it. I'm going to get Ed Jones, and have him come here and tell us how much it will cost to build a bedroom on the north. That thing can stand there until he can build it. We need another bedroom anyway."

And he was gone.

The bathtub stood where he left it for three weeks. That was when we began to build around, over, and under the original house.

8 Water and Other Weather

At last, in 1902 we began an active plan for water. "The
Woodward Water and Mining Company" was formed and the
names of nearly every man, woman, and child in town were
appended as stockholders. But that, alas, was about as far as the
company ever got.

Many of us had cisterns. When Mr. Laune had a pipe leading
from our cistern on the other side of the house to a pitcher pump

He wrote the metropolitan papers and his articles were published with favorable editorial comment. We ate and slept to the refrain of conservation and irrigation, until, in desperation I suppose, other men in the town allowed themselves to be drawn into the project. Twice he used his own money to finance the surveys, but at last he got a paper signed by other businessmen authorizing a third survey to which they all subscribed funds.

In 1904, a National Irrigation Congress met in El Paso, Texas. He and Mr. Cline were selected as delegates. On their return, Mr. Laune was more enthusiastic than ever about the possibilities of developing the water supply that was going to waste in the country. And—quoting from his report—"while it was decided at the National Convention to push work on the Mountain Park Project, I believe a dam across Beaver Creek can be built with the appropriation for Oklahoma if we come alive to the importance necessary to prevent the diversion of our funds by other states."

Though no immediate results came from his pleas, he continued to make them and went on working privately, spending his own limited money, hoping the time would come when practical and tangible results would follow.

After Mama, with Fritz and Fan, came from Nebraska, she and Mr. Laune began to look around for homesteads on which to file. Most of the land in the county had been claimed and we drove Flora and Fauna for miles looking for a location that would be desirable, yet not too far from town. We wanted adjoining claims if possible, where we could live beside each other until we could "prove up," and at last we found what we thought would suit our purpose, about five and a half miles west of town.

An old neighbor had watched our search with interest. When we took him out to look at the land we had selected, he stooped and took a handful of the soil in his gnarled old hand, squeezed it into a ball, and watched it crumble slowly.

"That's a sign of good land, Mr. Laune," he declared. "If you squeeze it, and it stays squz before it falls apart, it's good soil."

I smiled, for invariably, when we went into the yard or a field, Mr. Laune did what the old man had done; scooped a handful of the earth into his hand, squeezed it and watched it crumble.

It did not look like very good soil to me. Hard, bright red, with patches of sand here and there. The Indians had a saying that "he who gets the dust of red earth on his feet, can never be free to roam again. No matter where, or how far he wanders, the red-earth will draw him back, for red-earth will hold you 'til you die."

The land we chose was typical of the country, gently rolling prairie land covered with buffalo grass. There was a creek cutting across a corner of Mama's claim, bordered with scrubby elms, cottonwoods, and willows. On a high ridge that we called the "hog-back," we found quantities of oyster shells. This mystified me. Oyster shells on the high prairies? Mr. Laune explained that in some far-distant past this had been an ocean bed.

When we made filings, he joked about betting Uncle Sam that we could live on the place five years without starving to death. If we won, Uncle Sam would give us the land, "free, gratis, for nothing," and a title—or patent—to it. If we failed to keep our contract, but stayed on the place eighteen months, we could have the land by paying a dollar an acre. Mama won her bet, and at the expiration of five years was granted a patent to the place; but we lived on ours only eighteen months and paid the required dollar an acre.

A lot of people cheated Uncle Sam. They filed on the land, built a soddy or shanty, or dugout, plowed a few furrows, visited the place occasionally, and swore to having made residence. Sometimes such claims were contested. Somebody who wanted that land or just didn't like the person who filed produced witnesses who swore that the claimant had not acted in good faith and had not met the requirements of the law. If the contention could be proved before the Land Office Commission, and the original filing was cancelled, then the contestant, or someone else, could file on it. Some claims were bitterly contested, even to the point of shooting it out, but this did not happen often.

As soon as we made filings, Mama began to prepare to move out and begin her residence. There was a small country school nearby, but it was soon moved onto Mama's claim. She gave an acre of her land for this purpose. The school was adequate for Fan, but Fritz stayed in town with us until it was time for us to move on our claim. The law allowed us six months after filing before it was obligatory for us to start our residence, and we were going to take advantage of this leeway.

At last, we began to make preparations for moving to our claim house which squatted low and broad on a slight knoll near the line where Mama's house stood.

We rented our house and Mr. Laune rented a room in town where he stayed during the week. We found an excellent man to do the work on the claim and look after us. There were congenial neighbors with whom we became fast friends. We organized a Sunday School, and I taught a class of young people, and it was fun. They sometimes met at my home on Saturday evening and we made candy and practiced the songs for the next day. Mama and I would sometimes "spend the day" with our neighbors and they returned the visits, while we exchanged recipes, quilt patterns, and sewed, crocheted, and chattered. And we went to town quite often, driving Dixie and Yankee, a wonderful team I will have more to say about later.

As Mr. Laune could not be with us except over Sunday, perhaps after all we did not make true residence on our claim, for a lot of time the children and I were on the road going to, or coming from, town. We had a buggy with a roomy compartment at the rear in which to carry supplies, which was covered with a leather hood to protect the contents from the weather. One wild windy day, the box held a new hat I had just bought in town. I suspect I didn't fasten the hood securely. I thought I saw a tumbleweed sail past my head, but when I went to show Mama my new hat, it was gone. I knew then that it was no tumbleweed I had seen.

I never saw or heard of that lovely hat again. I tried to comfort myself with the hope that a nice Eskimo lady would like it when it reached the far north. And from the speed it was going when I saw it, I thought it would be there quite soon.

The children were entranced with the claim. A sandy hill, which we called "Sugar Loaf Mountain," rose on our place, and on it, and in the draw, grew beautiful wild flowers—Spanish daggers, or more poetically, "Candles of the Lord," flaming Indian paintbrush, blue lupines, wild verbena, horse-mint, crocuses, primroses, and star-of-the-evening. We gathered them, and our houses were beautified by them.

Almost as soon as we filed on our land Mr. Laune had a grove of little trees planted in a corner of the place. We had a well dug, and a windmill and water tanks put up. The well produced "Gyp" water; we were not unfamiliar with that.

In about a year, a man came to see us and offered to find us a well of "sweet water." He went to the trees on Mama's creek and cut a forked branch that he whittled down to a sharp V, which he called a "divining rod." I don't know what tree the branch came from or if the "magic" will work from just any kind.

Grasping the two ends of the fork in his hands with the sharp end sticking straight up, he marched over the place. The theory was that when he came to a place where "sweet water" was hiding deep in the ground the stick would turn over and point down to it. Around and around he walked, in the draws, over the knoll, up and over Sugar Loaf, with our entire family, and Jack, following. At one place, each time we approached, the stick would turn a little.

Then it happened. The stick turned over and pointed down. The man's knuckles were white, and the stick cracked, but down it came, slowly, and definitely.

Mopping his brow, the man panted, "Here it is, Mr. Laune. You'll find 'sweet water' right here."

And we did!

It almost makes me cross when people ask, "Do you believe that a stick could tell where soft water was located?" but I don't argue about it. We got soft water without a taint of gypsum.

And without going to China for it, either. I don't know how it happened. But I don't know how the moon and the stars happen to stick close to the sky—or wherever they do stay. That has nothing to do with the fact that they are there to bless us. I just don't argue about miracles.

I was delightfully surprised when Mr. Laune gave me a rubber-tired Stanhope. It had no top, and the back of the high seat curved gracefully up and up. On this high seat I perched proudly like a robin on a weathervane. But, unlike the buggy, there was no nice roomy floor and no wide protected seat on which to park the children. I sat in the middle, with a child on each side, their arms linked through mine for safety.

Returning from town one day when I could scarcely see the road through the curtain of blowing sand, Paul bounced from the seat beside me and hurtled out into the air. With one lightning-like movement, I snatched his overcoat and held him tight against the side of the buggy until the horses stopped. Then I dragged him up, frightened but unhurt, into the seat. He was a husky child, and only about an inch of his collar was left attached to his overcoat. In grabbing for Paul I unseated Russell and almost lost her on the other side. Right then I decided that the Stanhope was designed for solo, or adult duet; certainly not for family service.

That summer was terribly hot, the kind of weather that breeds tragedies. A mother of two children who lived on a farm, had taken her pallet out into the yard one night to try to find cooler air. Her husband found her the next morning lying quiet and cold in a welter of blood; she had cut her throat. It caused a wave of sympathetic horror over the county. People said the country was "Hard on the womenfolks." Later on, plans were formed to provide a place in town where the women who had to come long miles for supplies could gather and rest or visit, so that the monotony of their lives on the isolated claims and farms could be broken.

The despair of this other mother of two children and her tragic death may have had something to do with Mr. Laune's willingness to let me take the children for a visit to Texas. At any rate, I had been away about two weeks, and was having a wonderful time with all my friends in Clarendon and Wellington, when I received the *Woodward News* with this item marked with a blue circle:

> Mrs. S. B. Laune and the children are visiting friends in Clarendon, and other nearby Texas points. This is the way S. B. feels as he eats alone in the hotel. And this is what, in his loneliness he wrote:
>
> > The hot sand doth blow,
> > And when shall we know
> > When the blistering wind will turn back;
> > She packed up her grip, and away she did go,
> > While the dear one at home, holds the sack.

I thought that if "the dear one at home" felt that way, I'd better pack my grip and hurry back to him.

However, I was not very well, and it was still very hot. Mr. Laune decided to take me to Colorado, but before we left, I suddenly realized that I had not had the children baptized. It worried me, though why I thought it was more important to have them baptized because I was going to leave them for a little while, I don't know. When I talked to their father about the matter, he was beautifully indifferent. His church, the Christian Church, did not think infant baptism at all important. In fact, he did not believe in it at all. I was a member of the Methodist Church and thought it a parent's duty to have children baptized.

"Why, of course, honey, if it will make you any happier, have them baptized," he agreed amiably. "It won't hurt them to have water sprinkled on their heads. Might even do them a little good, hot as it is. Sure, you go ahead and have them baptized." Having voiced this big-hearted agreement, he resumed his paper.

"I can't have them baptized unless you stand with me and take the vows, too. You're their father. You have to do that."

This was something he was utterly unprepared for. He turned shocked, betrayed eyes on me. "Aw no, honey!" Then, because

whole world. If he had told us anything at all I had not comprehended it; I had been too busy making a fuss of my own. Docility is not my most outstanding virtue, so I heaved and dragged the lower door open, pushed on the trap door with my head, arms, and shoulders, and finally we emerged, covered with dust and cobwebs.

Mr. Laune was strolling about the yard, gazing at the sky with a look of deep satisfaction on his face. The cyclone blew itself out before it got to Oklahoma.

The angel-food cake was all right.

It was after the children and I had moved back to town, that a cyclone swept over the section where we had our claims. Mama saw it coming. A great black cloud, twisting and tumbling. She saw the long white tail reach down to the earth, slashing and whipping over the land. The man who was working for us urged Mama to run for the storm-cave, but just then she saw the tail pick up a neighbor's claim shanty (fortunately the owner was away) and come sailing with it directly toward her house. She stood in the open doorway, waving her hands, and shouting commandingly: "Don't you dare drop that house down on my garden!"

Again Mr. Harvey implored her to run. "Don't be absurd; do you think for a single minute that I shall leave my house for that cyclone to tear up?" she told him.

He stayed beside her, unwilling to leave her alone in the path of death. He watched in silent awe as the cloud dipped over the garden, lifted, dipped again and—smashed the little house down just outside the garden fence. . . .

Not a bean in Mama's garden was disturbed.

9 Clubs and I

The ladies of the town, dressed in the height of fashion, leaving engraved calling cards and in every detail following the social customs of metropolitan society, had been prompt to call when I first arrived and invite me to all the parties and receptions. We were quickly drawn into the Shakespeare Club that Mr. Laune had helped to organize almost as soon as he washed his hands after driving the stake on his lot, and I was asked to become a member of the Coterie Club. This was the second federated club in Oklahoma Territory. Most of the members were older than I, and were so competent, so gaily determined that Woodward should be a cultural center, and—I thought—so intellectual, that

145

I was overwhelmed by the honor of being asked to become a member. I hesitated about joining, as I didn't see how I could find time to spare, but Mr. Laune insisted I needed the stimulation that this club offered.

It was, and is, a remarkable organization in ways beyond its constitutional definition of "a literary, charitable, and sociable" association. It really set the standards and formed the social policies of the town. The rigid rules that forbade gossip of any kind, politics in a partisan sense, and religion from a denominational standpoint, though "unwritten laws," were so consistently observed that the closest harmony has prevailed right up to the present time. No words of mine can express what a factor this club has been in the enrichment of my life.

We met in alphabetical order and, as the houses were so small, it was frequently necessary for the hostess to move beds and other large pieces of furniture out into the yard to make room for the meetings. Some of us were obliged to sit on the floor; I, with a baby on each side of me. Years later, I heard one of our sons say that the reason he did not attain a desired height of six feet, was because his growth was stunted from having to sit on the floor at Coterie meetings, unable to stretch out his legs or even take a deep breath.

For some time, Coterie had felt the necessity of a Library in the town, and with eighty dollars, earned by a Fourth of July celebration, in the treasury it seemed like a good time to start one. Mrs. Patton, the doctor's wife, said she would write Mr. Andrew Carnegie who, she had read, was founding libraries all over the country. And she would write to Mr. John D. Rockefeller, who had a lot of money, too. She thought they would be glad to furnish Woodward with a library if they were asked. The other eighteen members thought this was a good idea, and it was moved, seconded and carried, that Mrs. Patton write and tell these wealthy gentlemen that the Woodward Coterie Club would appreciate it very much if they would furnish sufficient funds to open a circulating library in Woodward.

She wrote, and the club members waited impatiently for a reply. It came. Mr. Carnegie, or the committee that received requests in his name, had received our letter and noted contents, but respectfully begged to advise the club that it was not the policy—and so forth. It was a nice letter, but, briefly, Woodward was too small for a Carnegie library fund. Mr. Rockefeller wrote and said he was not giving out libraries at all.

Coterie was not discouraged. With eighty dollars, we would just go ahead and start the library ourselves. Margaret Gerlach rose in meeting and said she thought it was time to stop talking about it, and go to work on a real program. She contributed a book by Richard Carvel and then each of us gave a book, so the library had eighteen books right away.

Our county clerk offered to let us use the rear shed room of the shack that was his office. This room, unfinished except for a floor, and with only two small windows, was on the west side. In summer the sun beat down mercilessly on the sloping roof, and in the winter it was freezing cold.

With our eighty dollars, we sent away for more books. The members of Coterie "took turns alphabetically," in keeping the library open for the patrons who paid a dollar for a membership card. We began a series of pie-suppers, food sales, chicken dinners, and such things to make money to buy more books. Citizens of the town became interested and a number of books were donated.

After a while, the city decided that the library should be a municipal affair, and bought it from us. We were happy to turn it over to them. After another while, Mr. Carnegie came through with his help and the town acquired a Carnegie Library.

The study program of Coterie for those years was enough to stagger busy mothers and housekeepers. We studied every country in the world, beginning with the very first records that we could find. When our third child was a nursing baby, I read two thick volumes of Greek history aloud to him because I had to give a paper on the subject, and this was a way to satisfy the other children's cry, "Read to us!" at the same time. Mr. Laune said he suspected that no other baby had been nurtured on Greek history at such a tender age.

Our own country was studied carefully from the discoveries,

on down through the colonizations to the Revolution. Then we read aloud at the meetings every word of the Constitution and Amendments, and such controversial writings as we could find. These included writings of the Adamses, Franklin, Washington, and others. We invited lawyers and teachers in the town to come and give us more intelligent interpretations than we could form of some of the questions involved.

Once a year, we rewarded our husbands for the help that they so willingly gave our every endeavor, with a banquet. This was the high point in the year.

At that time, there were no fast refrigerated cars, automatic refrigerators, or even many iceboxes. We were forced to send away to Wichita, Kansas—the nearest market—for fresh fruits and vegetables, such as head-lettuce, artichokes, mushrooms, and alligator pears. We gave one of the banquets at the hotel, on Washington's Birthday. We sent away for ice cream molded in the form of George and Martha. Huge chrysanthemums were favors for the ladies, and there were small button chrysanthemums for the men's lapels. We had hand-painted place cards and menus, music and speeches and toasts. It was the last word in epicurean elegance.

At about the same time I became a member of Coterie, I was asked to join the Social Club, which met for the sole purpose of having a good time. We took our embroidery, darning, or other hand work. We had no charitable obligations and did nothing for the "uplift of the town." We simply relaxed and remembered that we were young. Later, the club was turned into a card club and so remains to this day.

The people of the town were seldom bored. For one thing, unusual musical talent was discovered almost as soon as there *was* a town. Len Stine, who ran a wholesale liquor business, recognized the need for something that would provide entertainment for the town and interest for some of the young men. So he invested $450.00 in instruments for a town band, and acted as leader until he found someone he thought more competent. In no time at all, concerts were being held on Main Street corners,

and the band played for all public occasions. If the band lacked
something in the way of harmony and technique, it made up for
all deficiencies in volume of sound. Anyway, people were not
critical, but appreciative. It was wonderful to see the young men
tooting and blowing and puffing, their cheeks swelled to balloons
and their eyes bulging. Quartettes, male, female and mixed, were
formed and sang cheerfully for every kind of entertainment as
well as for church and the rare funeral services. A music club
was formed that included those who loved to listen as well as
those who participated. But even in a music club where nearly
everything is donated, money is necessary. At least, a little
money.

The club therefore voted that each member should give a dollar
to defray unavoidable expenses. Since not everyone could afford
to give a dollar right out of her husband's pocket, it was decided
that the dollar must be earned. Some husbands declared that the
earning of the dollar cost them far more than that amount, and
pled with their wives just to give the dollar and forget it.

A certain woman's husband—you guess which one—broke forth
in plaintive verse which his wife found pinned to her pillow one
morning:

> Oh, please just take a buck from me,
> I do not want again to be
> Compelled to earn some money.
>
> I'll gladly give a dollar now,
> That I will steal, or get somehow;
> But let's don't "earn" it, honey.

Hank O'Brian was not one of the husbands who protested. He
had turned so many ice-cream freezer cranks, had driven so
many miles collecting and returning so many dishes and chairs
and tables, had wiped so many dishes after the parties, that a little
thing like helping his wife, Stasia, earn a dollar for the music club
was duck soup for him. When Stasia explained the matter to
Hank, he was ready.

"What about that melon patch I have across the track?" he

asked, lazily. "Why not peddle watermelons? They're wonderful watermelons. Everybody likes watermelons. Y'oughta make a dollar."

"Will you help me?" asked Stasia, guilefully. Stasia knew, and everyone in town knew, that Hank would help Stasia do anything, if she asked him. He would help, he agreed, by driving the wagon to the field, by gathering the ripe melons, by loading them into the wagon, and driving to the customers that Stasia solicited, and dumping them on porches or in kitchens. Of course, Stasia would go along for the ride. One thing Hank made clear, he would *not* drive up and down the street hollering, "Watermelons for sale." Stasia had to do that, if it was done at all. And he wouldn't go into the stores and drum up the trade.

Stasia promised. Hank drove up and down Main Street, grinning broadly while Stasia went in and out of the stores, and piped in her treble voice, "Watermelons for sale."

She made one dollar and sixty cents.

Several years later, in 1914, I was asked to prepare the charter for a P.E.O. chapter in our town. This invitation came to me through a friend, Minnie Olmsted, in the near-by town of Waynoka, where there was an active chapter. Not knowing anything about this P.E.O. except that it is the largest women's organization in the world independent of a related men's organization, and is international in scope, I blithely agreed to form a chapter. I chose those members of Coterie whom I knew inside and out. There were a few other names added, and throughout all the years since then the chapter has worked and played and grown.

People often ask, "What is this P.E.O.? What does it mean?"

When we were organizing our chapter and I was dipping into my husband's very shallow pockets every now and then for one thing and another connected with the first meeting, he said that it meant, a "Pretty Expensive Order." Others said, when they learned that the membership of a chapter was limited to a small group, that the initials stood for a "Pretty Exclusive Order." Those are as good answers as any. . . .

P.E.O. was organized in 1869 by seven girls, students at Iowa Wesleyan College in Mt. Pleasant, Iowa, and now, in the middle of the twentieth century, has a membership of almost one hundred and twenty thousand.

Our P.E.O. Chapter in Woodward, through the interest of one of its members, Myra Root, in a blind young girl of our town, began a movement in the 'twenties that for a few years surprised and delighted us with the response from other chapters not only in Oklahoma, but in many of the other states.

The plan Mrs. Root presented to our chapter was not only to give reading matter to the sightless, but work to trained but idle hands. We wanted money to be paid to blind transcribers, for there were many who were skilled in transcribing, but who could not get the work to do, for lack of money in the National Library for the Blind treasury. So they sat in darkness and idleness with nothing to do and nothing to read, for they soon exhausted the scant supply of matter available. When the State Convention of P.E.O. was held in Woodward in 1927, we solicited the help of all the chapters in the state. We introduced the battle cry, "Let Every Chapter Give A Book For The Blind," and many chapters in many states took up the challenge.

A committee was appointed with Mrs. Root as the chairman, and worked for five years through the various chapters and their members, and a few outside friends. In those five years, we gave work to blind transcribers who had been sitting in idle and perpetual darkness. Seventy books, besides numerous short stories and articles were given to the National Library for the sightless. Congress, importuned, raised their appropriation to $70,000.00, the Pratt Bill was passed and the Library of Congress received $100,000.00 for having books embossed.

That was a fine movement as it gave more books to be read; but it did not help those who wanted work, and were ready to give skilled service in transcribing. Helen Keller wrote us, "Remember that the transcribing of books into Braille gives the blind a means of self-support as well as the joy of reading."

The depression may have had something to do with the discontinuance of this work through the P.E.O. Chapters but the real reason was the interest of the international, or Supreme officers, in what they considered a larger work and more in line with the policy of the sisterhood; this centered in Cottey College, which they own, in Nevada, Missouri, and the Educational Loan Fund to aid girls aspiring to further their education.

But after all, most important, the objectives had been reached; appropriations had been increased, and a consciousness had been aroused as to the need of an interest in the work for the sightless.

To jump way ahead of my story, after having served on the executive board of Oklahoma State P.E.O. I was elected State President for 1920-1921. I was overwhelmed with this honor and the duties and responsibilities it entailed, but I was fortunate in having the generous help of my predecessors, and the association of many fine women. Through this channel, my acquaintance over the state was extended and it all proved to be a most rewarding and happy experience, instead of the arduous task I had feared.

When I occasionally hear people today ridicule the "American clubwoman" I just think to myself, "You don't know what you are laughing at." Certainly, Woodward would have been a very different town—and not as good—if there had been no women's clubs, and my life, to speak only for myself, would have been infinitely poorer.

10 So Much Good in the Worst— and Vice Versa

Nineteen hundred was a good year for Republicans. McKinley was re-elected to the Presidency. Dennis Flynn of Kansas, who, ever since his first election to Congress in 1892, had been trying to secure the passage of the Free Homes Bill, had at last seen it signed by the President, and thereby the settlers were relieved of making further payments on their homesteads—a measure which, it was said, "created a surplus of ready cash and gave thousands of families their first financial breathing spell since the opening of the strip."

Mr. Laune was elected prosecuting attorney of Woodward County.

The county officers were still occupying small shacks scattered along Tenth Street, just off of Main. In May, Judge Burford, the district judge, called on the Grand Jury to investigate the need for a county courthouse and jail.

Maybe others beside Mr. Laune were engaged in working on the new courthouse after the contracts had been let and work begun, but it seemed to me he was building it unaided and alone. When water flooded the newly dug basement, Mr. Laune was distracted. He ate and slept with the worry of that water, and all but took up permanent residence on the edge of the excavation. When that matter was safely negotiated and the basement as dry as a powder horn, there were the walls to fuss over. I accused him of spending his days with a plumb line and level affixed to the walls. "They must be straight; they've *got* to be straight," he went about muttering to himself.

At last the courthouse was completed, and the people of the county had a good building. The paper proclaimed: "We now have the finest courthouse in Northwest Oklahoma, with spacious halls, a double stairway, ample offices and courtroom."

When the officers moved in at last, Mr. Laune was thin, but proud.

Soon after taking office as prosecuting attorney, an old client, Mr. Dreiling, came out to the house one night to see Mr. Laune. He was enraged because of the encroachment he claimed one of his neighbors was making on his pasture.

"But the surveyor's markings clearly show the boundaries of your property, Sol," Mr. Laune soothed. "All you have to do is stay within your own border, and Mr. Blank will stay within his. No need for you to have any trouble."

A few days later, complaints were made that Mr. Dreiling was trespassing on his neighbor's property, and there was going to be trouble. The parties were sent for and a hearing of the case was held. As no amicable agreement was reached, the court ordered the surveyor to go back and with both men present run the lines again. However, Mr. Dreiling was still belligerent and had to be put under a peace bond.

In another little while a complaint was made that Mr. Dreiling had removed the surveyor's stones and carried them to points that pleased him better. A warrant was issued for his arrest, and the sheriff brought him in. It was hard for Mr. Laune to convince his former client that he was no longer free to represent him in this matter, that he represented the county, and would certainly do his best to punish any infringement of the law.

Mr. Dreiling was put in jail.

He made a cheerful inmate. He was an energetic worker and was soon suggesting changes to improve and beautify the courthouse grounds. Finally, the jailer asked that he be released from confinement to carry out some of his plans. He was cheery and apparently happy as he worked at will on the odd jobs he found to do.

One day, he asked to be paroled to go to his farm over the weekend. It was during the growing season, and there was much to be done on the farm where his wife and children, with the occasional help of a neighbor, were doing the work.

The parole was granted and Mr. Dreiling started the long walk home.

We were having breakfast Sunday morning, when the sheriff rode up to the door and called Mr. Laune out. I do not remember whether Mr. Dreiling had returned to the jail in Woodward alone, or in company with a neighbor, but he had calmly announced that when he reached home in the early dawn on Saturday he had killed a man who was in the field with Mrs. Dreiling, where they said they had gone to drive the hogs out of the crops.

The case was set to come up in the fall, and because of the feeling against Mr. Dreiling, a change of venue was taken from Woodward to a near-by county. The state declared it murder in the first degree; the defense, that Mr. Dreiling had acted in defense of the honor of his home.

As he grew better, and it was necessary to feed him oftener, I found Birdie scraping the steak with the edge of a spoon until only the fibre remained. This pulp, after a light seasoning, she spread between thin slices of whole-wheat bread, and he ate the small sandwiches with relish. We did not tell him the meat was raw.

Birdie continued to help me with the work after Mr. Laune was well enough to return to the office. Each morning the children watched eagerly to see her come, in her soldier hat and coat, squared back on the tiny seat of the sulky, her feet spread wide and her toes braced against the shafts. Old gray Mollie pounded spiritedly down the street to the carriage block where she drew up with a flourish.

I don't know where Birdie got Mollie and the sulky. Mollie, in her young days, had been a racing trotter. She had a proud lift to her head, and a light still shone in her bright old eyes. She seemed to retain memories of the days when her limbs had been fleet and crowds cheered her as she dashed past the grandstand.

The house was shining and the children were taking their afternoon naps the day Birdie told me how she got her claim.

"I was overseeing the dance hall one night," she said, "and it made me sicker and sicker. And madder and madder. The girls didn't have pretty clothes. Just shabby, cheap old things; and girls in that business need pretty clothes. If they don't have them, it all looks so—so—" she searched for a word, "—common. But the men didn't have any money. It was the cheapest kind of joint, I tell you.

"And me. I wasn't used to any such place. I was swearing mad to think I was mixed up in such a place. I had letters asking me to come to St. Louis, and a fine place in Kansas City, and they would pay my way there. But I was sick and tired of the whole business.

"And I said out loud: 'God, get me out of this place; get me out of this business. I want a home of my own, and I'll do whatever You say, if You will get me a place of my own.'

"Do you believe in prayer—that God answers prayer?" she turned to ask me.

I nodded.

"Well, there was a man there in the hall, watching. He had just come to town. He wasn't dancing, or drinking, much. He looked over at me and grinned when he heard me swearing to God. He didn't say anything then, but after I locked the hall he kept hanging around, and he said: 'Did you mean that you just want to get into a higher-class place in this business? Just what kind of place of your own do you want?'

"And I said: 'Mister, I'm so sick to death of this whole business, and this kind of mess, I could die. I've got letters asking me to come to other places, but I haven't got the stomach for this life, any more.'

"'Well,' he said, 'if it's just a piece of land of your own you want, I know where you can get a claim to file on. It's sorta covered up with fences, and some of the people around there want to keep it covered up, but if you're in earnest, and want to work hard—and I mean, hard—I'll take you out there tomorrow and you can look it over.'

"That was Saturday night.

"I asked him: 'Say, if this place can be filed on, how come you don't file on it?' And he said:

"'My wife is dead, and I have a little girl in Kansas, staying with my folks. I came out here with the thought of filing, but I can't bring her here and live on a claim with her alone.'

"And I said, 'All right, brother, if you want to do a good turn without pay, I'll borrow a horse and buggy, and tomorrow we'll drive out and look at this land.'

"He was waiting at the Blue Front Livery Barn the next morning. We drove past the church and folks were going along all dressed up. He pulled his hat down and I thought he was trying to hide his face. 'What's the matter, 'fraid folks'll see you riding with me?' I asked him. He just laughed.

"We drove out, and the land, like he said, was pocketed in between claims on both sides. All under fence. But it looked good to me. There was a creek running near. I wanted to get out of the buggy and kiss the earth. I asked him to keep quiet, and not mention it to anybody until I could get my filing papers. He said he was leaving town on the next train.

"Early Monday morning, I went to town. No one was suspicious of anything unusual, because I always went to town Monday, to do the buying for the house.

"I went directly to the land office and told the clerk, who I knew, all about everything. I didn't hold anything back. I told him I wanted a home of my own, my very own, that I had worked and paid for, myself.

"He was mighty kind, and helped me make my filing. And I started in to play square with the Lord. And the Lord?" She laughed. "Well, He moves in a mysterious way, like the Bible says." She chuckled again. "I was a sinner," she pursed her lips and looked at me obliquely, "and He's tryin' me, sister, He's tryin' me."

Some of the people on neighboring claims were outraged that a woman with the brand of shame on her brow would dare to move among respectable folk and, for many long months, made a determined effort to drive her out. The precious wood was cut from the creek on her place. Fences were found down and the cattle got into her growing crops. The pasture was burned. However, there were some who understood her difficulties and gave her a helping hand, even showing her great kindness. They would have done more, but Birdie was stubborn and refused to ask for aid.

She would come to work some mornings almost distracted by the antagonism surrounding her. She sat limp and white after walking in to town. She had to walk now, because one sad day good, faithful Mollie had died in the little barn—a snug shelter of posts and wire and straw that Birdie had put up. Mollie had been more than a useful horse; she had been a companion and confidant, to whom Birdie could pour out her hopes and longings and fears.

She divided her pitiful earnings: a dime for food for herself, a nickle for the stray dog she had welcomed, the balance for food for the chickens and pig and calf, and a plank or post for the crude shack she was trying to build with her own hands. And the laundry, the feed, the plank or post, all had to be carried on her shoulders. Plank by plank, post by post, a nickel here and a dime there—everything went into the building of a home of her own. She grew so thin that as she said she had to stand twice to make a shadow.

Fanning her hot face with her soldier hat, she would sit exhausted, cuddling my babies on her knees. "Birdie's necessity is sure somebody's opportunity," she would say with her pixy grin. "I'm reading my Bible every day, like I promised God. I'm so tired; there's a lot I don't understand, but I keep reading. I didn't promise to understand. And if this is the way He wants it, I'll try to do His way. At least," she chuckled, "I'll try as long as my back and legs hold out."

She hired a neighbor to plow her field, and she sowed the grain herself, broadcasting the precious stuff with her small brown hands.

"I reckon I didn't really count the grains," she told me, "but I measured them mighty careful."

The crop came up and covered the field with a carpet of green velvet. She was jubilant. "I called that wheat up out of the ground, I did. I named the grains every one. And I prayed over them, and begged them to come up good and strong. The Lord heard my prayer, glory be, and they came up. God be praised! It's a beautiful field."

And then when she went home one evening, spent with weariness, she found cattle feeding in the field. A post had been broken and the wires of the fence fastened down so the cattle could enter.

"I nearly went crazy," she told me, her eyes bright with the tears she would not let fall. "I drove the stock out of the field, my lovely field, all trampled and ruined. I lifted up the post with the wires stapled to it, but it was broken. It wouldn't stand. I couldn't leave it that way, because the cattle would come back. I went to the creek and hacked down a sapling to make another post. But I couldn't dig a hole. My posthole digger was in town to be mended. I didn't know what to do, but I had to fix that fence.

"So I said, 'All right, God, I don't think You are playing fair, but I haven't always played fair with You. Maybe You are chastening me. I'll fix that fence, if I have to dig the hole with my tongue.'

"After thinking and hunting all around, all I could find to dig with was a long-handled, steel kitchen spoon. The ground was as hard as concrete. After a long while, and after I kept wetting the earth with a little water, I got a little hole started. I kept on, until it was deep enough to hold the post. It's pretty hard sometimes, sister, pretty hard.

"I know who does the meanness to me," she said wearily. "They're respectable people, folks who go to church," her lips curled in scorn, "the best Society. Maybe friends of yours. But I'm not going to tell who they are until I get my land proved up. And then I'll tell. That is," she grinned crookedly, "if I can still talk."

In late spring, she reported, "When I went home last night, I found a note stuck in my door. It said: 'The south corner has been plowed and sowed to kaffir. Good luck and keep your chin up.'"

And for the first time, I saw her weep.

"There are men still tramping the sod," she gulped, "made in the image and likeness of God. Good men, and decent. I'm sorry I've hated all of them."

At the end of five years, Birdie did prove up her land, but by that time her "respectable" neighbors were her friends.

One evening I was expecting Fan to come in town and take care of the children so we could go to a Coterie party. But in the afternoon the clouds that had been gathering in the northwest changed to the southwest. There was an ominous greenish cast to the sky; and on the divide south of town hung a peculiar cone-shaped cloud that we watched anxiously.

This cloud burst about a mile south of town. I learned later that a stream of water was sent down the valley and Main Street, flowing into the stores, and taking everything before it. By the time the water reached the center of town it had gained enough force to sweep the harness shop and a restaurant down the street and strand them against the Santa Fe tracks. Two hundred yards of track washed from the roadbed, and for miles up and down the line the damage was severe, delaying all trains for thirty-six hours. The thunder and lightning were so terrifying that I was thankful to be at home with the children and not at any party. I took my book into the bedroom where the children were sleeping calmly through the turmoil, wishing with all my heart that Mr. Laune were with me, but he had been caught by the storm at his office.

To shield the children from the light I put the lamp on the floor and sat beside it, leaning my back against the wall beneath the window, where I sat shivering and shaking and trying to read. Suddenly there came a pounding on the window beside my head, and a shouting almost in my ears. I turned, and froze in horror to see the wild-eyed face of a woman not an inch from mine.

"Let me in," she shouted, so loudly I could hear her quite plainly. "You tell Mr. Laune to come right out here and get me and my children out of that dugout. We're drowning."

The rain streamed down the windowpane, and she beat against the glass until I was afraid she would break it. I knew if the children should awaken and see her they would go into spasms of fear.

I opened the kitchen door and the wind blew her inside, the water draining from her clothes, making little rivulets on the floor.

As soon as she got inside, and while I was struggling with all my strength to close the door, she began to swear. With chattering teeth, she cursed me, Mr. Laune, and the children. I was so scared and surprised I could hardly stand. Closing the bedroom door so she would not waken the children, I assumed a calmness that amazed me.

"Who are you?" I demanded. "And where did you come

11 Progress on All Fronts

Some time fairly early in the new century—I don't remember the exact year—the part of town known as East Woodward began a vigorous campaign to have the town incorporated. It was pointed out that for years the town had been governed by county officers, and people in East Woodward were tired of it. They also wanted waterworks, so they could have fire protection and street sprinklers, they wanted the streets properly named, better sidewalks, a telephone system and electric lights.

There were some insulting pieces in the paper about the condition of the streets. The Board of Health was urged to do something about the manure pile in front of the post office, almost in the middle of Main Street. The manure was not deliberately piled in the street; it just seemed to overflow from the livery stable and barn across from the post office.

People also wanted something done about a hole that became a deep mudhole after a rain, though at other times it was just a sun-cracked indentation. It was facetiously called "Uncle Jake's swimming pool," because it was in the street between Mr. Jake Thomas's drugstore and the Gerlach Bank. The paper ran a sarcastic little item: "Except for timely assistance, one of our prominent citizens would certainly have been drowned in Uncle Jake's swimming pool the night of The Big Rain. [And that was true.] The town should provide life preservers to avoid such accidents."

East Woodward issued a warning that horses, pigs and cattle found roaming the streets would be taken up and impounded, and that the poundmaster would collect one dollar for each animal turned in before it would be released. This drastic action, it was explained, was necessary "because there are a few cows and horses running the streets that can climb into a wagon as easily as a boy, and no farmer's wagon can be left unguarded until he has disposed of his load. The citizens are determined to stop this nuisance."

We, ourselves, were sometimes guilty of violating the herd law, for on occasions our team Dixie and Yankee would break out of the home corral and go on a wild spree, racing madly up and down Main Street. They were perfectly gentle, but would allow no one to catch them except a member of the family. This made the marshal and his deputies furious. Several times Mr. Laune was called out of court, or his office, and told to get his blasted team and take them home. A few times, when Mr. Laune was not available, I was called.

There was another law with a fine attached, requiring that horses driven or ridden to town should be hitched to the hitching rack. However, I would wrap the lines around the whip stock, get out of the buggy or surrey, and leave the team unhitched while I shopped, or just visited. Our mayor, Mr. Hopkins, who was also manager of the Gerlach-Hopkins Mercantile Store, would see the team standing unhitched and go out and tie them for me. Then he would say, "Mrs. Laune, someday I'm not going to see those horses untied, and you're going to be hauled up before the court and have to pay a fine. *Please* tie them."

And I, who would never dream of deliberately breaking a law, would promise in all good faith. Actually, it was the horses themselves, not the law, that forced me to remember to tie them. I would take a surrey load of members to Coterie, or a party, and the team would be left before our hostess's house, unhitched, to stand all afternoon, in all kinds of weather. After they had waited as long as they deemed proper and necessary, they learned to turn quietly and go home. They would walk carefully through the streets, turn at the right corners, cross the railroad tracks, and go into the barn where they waited calmly for someone to unharness them. Meanwhile my carriage guests and I would have to walk home.

One year, on my birthday, Mr. Laune came home bearing a large paper sack that he handed me with a "Happy Birthday" wish. When I started to take it into my hands, the contents wiggled, and I was warned with a quick, "Be careful; don't drop it."

Peeping inside, I saw a small white baby pig! "An Improved Ohio White Chester," I was told.

It was such a cunning little thing, so clean and babyish, that we made it a bed in the kitchen, as the February weather was too cold to leave it outside alone in the barn. Soon it was running around the house like a kitten. As long as the children were close at hand, it played happily in the yard with them, but if they outran it, or got out of sight, it would run after them squealing in anguish.

We named it Marguerite, and we all became very fond of her. Perhaps it sounds odd to say that Marguerite made a most engaging pet. She tagged the children around all day, going with them to the neighbors, and snuggling down beside the dog and cat with cozy grunts when they took their naps. She soon learned where all the choicest plants were growing in our yard, as well as the neighbors', and hurried to uproot them. After a while, she didn't wait for the children, but went visiting on her own account. As she grew in size, she grew more neighborly, and more unpopular.

Frantic calls for help, such as, "Mrs. Laune, will you please come, or send the children, to get the pig out of my yard!" became dreadfully familiar.

We would take Marguerite home and again strengthen the pen that had finally been built for her.

Mr. Laune became embarrassed to meet the neighbors who chorused the refrain: "You know Mr. Laune, about that pig of yours . . . well, I hate to complain, but—"

The pen was made tighter and larger.

The marshal rode up to our door. "Mrs. Laune, I hate like everything to bother you, but that white pig of yours—well, we've got a complaint from one of your neighbors. Something must be done about it, Mrs. Laune, she's getting to be a public nuisance. I sure do hate to bother you—"

We were convinced that no pen we built would hold Marguerite, so proficient was she in digging out, climbing over or pushing through. Mr. Laune spoke to one of the butchers in town—not the one from whom we bought our meat. ("Because," he explained to me miserably, "I didn't want to run the risk of eating the poor thing.") He told this butcher, who did not know either me or the children, that if he was cruising around in our neighborhood, and saw a white pig—she had grown huge by this time—wandering around, to take her up. But, he warned the man, if any of the family were about, just drive away, and wait until some time when he saw her out alone.

The butcher must have told another man, though he never admitted it. Anyhow, one day when the children were playing in our very own yard, with Marguerite grunting contentedly near by, a wagon drove up and a stranger hopped out, walked up to the pig, that was as friendly as a puppy, placed a gun to her head, and shot her.

Well!

At last, after an eloquent appeal by Temple Houston, the town voted for incorporation.

Now we could make our own laws. Because of the high-toned aspects of some of the desired innovations, an appeal was made to Coterie as the known arbiter of propriety and decorum. The club was asked to devise some plan about what should be done regarding the horses, wagons and buggies left in the street in front of the Knights of Pythias Hall, on Eighth Street, a new, two-storey brick building. As we had so few two-storey brick buildings it did seem this one should have a better chance of being seen, instead of being surrounded by a kind of public wagon-yard.

We in Coterie thought so, anyway, and began to plan for a place where the farmers could be supplied with a hitching lot. We didn't want to discourage the farmers from coming to town, for then where would any of us be? Finally a nice place was found for the horses and wagons, with a rest room near by for their wives, and the Knights of Pythias Hall stood revealed in all its elegance.

The City Council also asked Coterie to help in keeping the sidewalks clean. As all the women wore long trailing skirts finished around the wide sweeping bottom with a "brush-braid," we entered into this campaign with enthusiasm. We felt especially strong about the men's habit of spitting on the sidewalks; we thought that should definitely be stopped. It took a bit of diplomacy and tactful training, but before too long the offenders learned to step to the edge of the board sidewalk and to deposit the long streams of brown liquid and their quids of tobacco into the dusty street.

And our policemen put on uniforms.

There were only two or three men on the "force," but they looked wonderful in their blue suits with white braid, brass buttons, helmets, and white gloves. The uniforms made a splendid showing on our streets. They were warm in winter, when the officers were proud to wear them. They were even warmer in summer, and then the force longed to join the shirt-sleeve brigade.

But the mayor and the other city officers were adamant. The city had bought those uniforms, and had no intention of having them hang in closets, while the policemen went about in shirt sleeves. So they issued a warning that the uniforms were to be worn at all times when the officers of the law were on duty, coats, helmets, gloves and all. How else was Woodward to impress people from other towns?

The red-light district was cleared away, but still there were thirteen saloons and only six or seven churches. To be sure, the saloonkeepers contributed liberally to the building of the churches and attended every chicken-pie dinner, supper and festival, besides donating to all other worthy causes, and apparently worked just as hard as anyone else to make the town a nice place in which to live. However, we all thought the saloons were a menace, even though there was no visible impropriety on the streets.

At least, not often.

It is true that there was gambling; some of the citizens imbibed somewhat too freely; cocks were fought in the pits back of the saloons; and cowboys from the near-by ranches sometimes celebrated high, wide and handsome when they came to town. Sometimes there was a shooting scrape that shocked us. But as a usual thing, to us who were not personally affected, there was nothing objectionable to be seen.

We had a neighbor, a cattleman, who, when not drinking, was a soft-spoken, courteous gentleman. However, on one Fourth of July, he and a newcomer in town had an argument that grew into a quarrel. A few nights later, when they met in a saloon, the trouble was resumed. Through the intervention of friends, explanations were given and they agreed to forget the unpleasantness. In order to seal this new bond, they stepped to the bar to pledge their friendship. Some movement, or word, led the cattleman to doubt the sincerity of his companion, and he whirled and accused him of starting to draw a gun. The other denied this, but the cattleman was not satisfied and whipped out his gun. In an instant, bullets were flying. The stranger ran out of the

"Well, I can't tell whether it's bad news for Johnson or not, but it's sure bad news for me," drawled the voice at the other end of the line. "You tell Johnson I've got a hound dog here at the express office, and she's had eight puppies. You tell him to come and get 'em; I ain't got anything to feed 'em with, and they're carryin' a whoppin' insurance."

The messenger was sent and arrived at the Johnson farm where he found the family having an ice-cream party, in which he joined. When the ice cream was eaten up, he remembered to tell them about the hound dog and her eight puppies. Mrs. Johnson regarded the message as distinctly bad news. She threw up her hands in despair. "That's the reason we left Missouri," she wailed. "My husband spent his time fox-hunting with the hounds; and now, with all these rabbits and coyotes to chase on the prairies, and nine hounds to chase 'em with, we'll never get any farming done."

The townsmen, while struggling with the problems of incorporation in order to get on to bigger and better things for the town like water, sidewalks, and electric lights, were acutely conscious that the town's prosperity depended on the farmers and cattlemen. Unless the farmers found a side crop to supplement the cash crops of wheat and livestock, the town could not expand. They held meetings to which they invited the farmers and made fine speeches to them about the advantages of experimenting with various new, or at least unfamiliar, grains and legumes. But farmers were obliged to move cautiously in this new country of long summers and limited rainfall, though the soil was very productive if properly farmed, and the speeches often seemed to fall on deaf ears.

Peter Martinson and his father had come into the country the day of the Opening, both riding a small black mule. Both men secured homesteads not too far from town, and Peter Martinson also secured a lot in town on Main Street. On his town lot, with the aid of the small black mule and a primitive mill, Peter began grinding feed, a practical business which developed into a feed and grocery store that has continued throughout the years.

While the other businessmen were fuming and talking about a cash crop, Mr. Martinson remarked that he and his father were cultivating a crop of castor beans which he thought was a profitable one for the country. Castor beans have a beautiful palm-like plant that is quite exotic in appearance, but there was some prejudice against them because they were poisonous to cattle; on the other hand, they were also deadly to gophers and moles. However, a few of the farmers followed Peter Martinson's advice to plant castor beans, and he contracted to buy their crop. He was soon forced to enlarge his warehouse and in a year or two shipped twenty-five carloads of eight hundred bushels each; it was a very profitable venture for everyone concerned.

Broomcorn, another crop that yielded abundantly, was the favorite among farmers, and Woodward became one of the largest broomcorn markets in the country. During the season, the hotels were filled with buyers and the wagons, holding six bales, each of which brought fifty-five dollars, came into town in trains, just as the cotton wagons do in the South, blocking Main Street for nearly a mile.

Mr. Laune, along with many others, had long sheds built near our house in which to shelter and store the bales he could not resist buying. Our children and their friends found that the bales were easily converted into barricades while playing cops and robbers, and made splendid forts and mountains from which to fight all the wars from Armageddon to the Spanish-American, using Ridpath's History (their favorite reading matter) as their guide.

As I remember, it was just as well the children derived some benefit from the broomcorn, because the market usually went down as soon as our sheds were filled.

But in spite of all the new ideas people kept sprouting, kafir corn remains, as it always was, the real salvation of the country. It was grown there from the very beginning, and even in the driest years there has never been a complete failure of this crop which furnishes feed for poultry as well as for livestock.

and had him baptized there. I was told that I was not "consistent," not even "orthodox." And no doubt this was true, but I was determined to do everything to rear my children in "the fear and admonition of the Lord." I was reared that way, and Mr. Laune agreed that it was a very good way.

"Always do whatever makes you happy," he advised, "and everything will be all right."

12 Horses and Other Critters

When Mama had first gone to her claim she had to have a team and buggy, and as Flora and Fauna were gentle and reliable, Mr. Laune turned them over to her and began looking about for a team to take their place.

A client who owed him a fee asked if he would take a pair of three-year-old fillies in payment. They were the type Mr. Laune preferred; deep bay, with black stocking feet, long heavy black manes and tails, and with a white star in their foreheads between

"I didn't," I denied. "I just knew that white line indicated a sort of calculating, cautious nature, and the name 'Yankee' seemed kind of appropriate. Naturally a Dixie would be nicer to have around, don't you think? But the two will learn to pull together, you know, and they're nice names."

He grinned and said something under his breath.

Dixie and Yankee became members of the family, but they never became a bit more alike than they were as three-year-olds.

Horses always played an essential part in our lives. Dixie and Yankee, while indispensable as a driving team, were both broken to saddle, and Dixie was swift and dependable. Both of the older children had their own riding ponies. Russell's was Blue, a small mouse-colored mustang, as quick as lightning, but as gentle as Dixie. Paul's was Nellie, a satisfactory pony for a young boy, but as she was not as fast as either Blue or Dixie, he rode one of them whenever the occasion permitted.

The children would promise to "be careful" before they started out, but soon the telephone would begin to ring, and some worried friend would cry, "Mrs. Laune, I don't want to frighten you, but the horses are running away with your children. I'm afraid they'll be killed." I learned to take such franic reports calmly. They would come pounding up the street, Russell's long curls streaming behind her in the wind, the horses running abreast, for neither would let the other get ahead.

But with Paul, riding became a business. His father expected the same performance from him as he did of an experienced bronc-buster, and would say proudly, "That kid can deliver the goods."

One day they were down in the sales corral inspecting some horses that had just been brought to town. "What do you think of them, Son?" he asked seven-year-old Paul as they sat on the top bar of the fence. "Do you think you could ride that fellow?" indicating one of the horses. Paul, timid among strangers and hating for his father to call attention to him, shook his head, meaning, "Don't speak so loudly," but Mr. Laune answered himself, "Of course you can." And almost before the child knew what was happening, he felt himself thrown onto the horse's back. The animal humped up, skittered to one side, gave a quick buck, and Paul sailed into the air.

There was a murmur of disapproval among the men who witnessed the incident. Mr. Laune ran to pick up his son, whispering as he brushed him off and ran a quick hand over him, "Are you hurt?" Tears were pretty close, but Paul shook his head.

"All right," said his father, fright, tenderness and pride in his voice, "I want you to get back on that horse and show those fellows. I know you can ride him."

Mr. Laune caught the horse, talked to him a minute as he stroked his mane, and again put Paul on him. This time the horse shied, but the boy held his seat. When he quieted the animal and had ridden him around the lot a few times, his father hugged him as he helped him to the ground and walked out of the corral with his son, the proudest man alive.

When Sidney Benton was two, I went again to Nebraska, this time for an operation on my back. Before I was married, I had been thrown from a horse and dragged; the damage had been aggravated by many imprudences since then. While I was away Mr. Laune bought a carload of horses and sent Paul with them to our farm for summer pasture. They had to be herded, and as Paul had grown to be an experienced man of ten, his father thought he was quite capable of handling the job.

I knew nothing about it until after my return. The people on the farm, Mr. and Mrs. Allen Walters, were wonderful to Paul during the weeks he boarded with them and took care of the horses. They had sons of their own about Paul's age, and perhaps it really was not as risky as I imagined.

"Why, Allen wouldn't have let anything happen to Paul," his father kept telling me impatiently, when I stormed that it was dreadful to send so young a child to perform a man's work.

Paul counts that summer as one of the pleasant episodes of his childhood. But just the same, I grew afraid to turn my back for fear his father would set the boy to doing some impossible task that to him seemed simple and sensible.

The worst, from my point of view, happened when Paul was about seventeen and working during the summer as night billing-clerk at the freight office. A friend of Mr. Laune's, a rancher in New Mexico, wrote that because of the drought there he was desperate for pasture and could he get his cattle on grass in the vicinity of Woodward for two or three months before sending them to market? He went on to explain that the cattle were longhorns, those big tough animals of Mexican origin which once had roamed the prairies by thousands.

I was horrified. I had thought longhorns were extinct. Certainly none of the ranchers I knew had ever worked with them. But Mr. Laune was fascinated by the idea of bringing in the last of the breed; and, anyway, he could never say No to the appeal of a friend. In spite of my vehement protests, the time of their arrival was set, though I continued vainly to hope that the "thirty-six hour" law—requiring cattle to be taken from the cars for feed and water within that span of time—might prevent the two hundred and fifty head consigned to Mr. Laune from being dumped into the Woodward stockpens.

The cattle arrived. Because of the gathering war clouds (the year was 1917), young men were difficult to find. Court was in session, which meant Mr. Laune was not free to leave town. Men who had promised to be on hand failed to materialize.

There was nothing to do but put the problem in Paul's lap.

Driving that herd out to pasture was a job for four men, at the least, but Paul and an old cowhand, Mr. Butler, managed it somehow. The country was desolate and sandy, with scattered scrub and shin oak, and at the moment rejoicing in a temperature of 100 degrees. About halfway to the pasture, where one might have supposed that weariness alone would long since have taken the sparkiness out of the most untamed spirit, a mail carrier in an ancient Ford created a crisis. Butler, riding point, rode ahead to ask the carrier to keep his engine turned off until the herd had passed. But, whether through nervousness, impatience, or sheer ignorance, the carrier cranked up the car before the herd had gone a hundred yards by him, and at the noise the cattle took off helter-skelter, over the prairie. Paul, riding drag and swing, was terrified that Butler was going to be trampled to death; when last seen before the dust closed in he was riding for his life with one foot drawn up from the stirrup to avoid the vicious horns sliding by him. Miraculously, he came through without a scratch.

After ten dreadful days (the main trouble, of course, being water, or the lack of it) the Carter Ranch agreed to take over the herd and for a couple of months we had a respite.

Then the day came when the herd had to be driven back to the pens in Woodward. Mr. Laune and Paul went down to help.

Cutting the longhorns from the Carter cattle was a nerve-racking task. Mr. Carter, growing old, mounted his cutting horse and showed those younger cowboys a thing or two. They drove the herd up out of the rough shin-oak-covered country into a level stretch of sagebrush. About a mile away to the left, could be seen a settler's house, windmill and water tanks. Paul, on that side of the herd, spurred on to veer the steers to the right, but it was a futile effort: the herd, with an uncanny sense, went straight for that water. Paul reached the tanks only a few moments before the steers and turned to fight them off with a scantling he had snatched from the windmill, but he was forced to jump his horse, now in danger of being gored, onto the low platform of the windmill, a rather flimsy refuge.

The screeching of the windmill, the blowing sand, the bawling cattle and clanging horns, the stamping, bared-teeth and flattened ears of the horse terrified by the almost overpowering crush of steers, the shouting and swearing of the men battling their way in from the rim of the herd, appeared to him, Paul told me later, as confused as any battle scene pictured in Ridpath's History of the World.

When that herd was finally delivered for shipping, everyone in the Laune family drew a deep breath of relief. Even our eleven-year-old, Sidney Benton, had had to take his turn helping care for the critters before the Carters took them over. As I look back on our varied experiences with four-legged animals, that is the only one I remember with no pleasure whatever!

13 Some Two-Legged Animals

Mr. Laune used to say that he didn't mind being told how to conduct a case in court, manage the children, or how to get along with his wife, but by golly, he wasn't going to have any man tell him how to break his horses. Sometimes a man hired to care for our horses tried it, however, without fatal results, but if a horse came in with blood on its mouth, showing that a rough hand had jerked the bridle bit, only a kind Providence and a quick prayer saved the culprit from a good deal more than a curt dismissal.

More often, as it turned out, the men saw eye to eye with Mr. Laune. There was, for instance, Dan, a young ranchman, who came to work for us for a few months at two different times because he needed extra money to develop his ranch. During one winter when there was not much he could do on his own place, he left his young wife and little boy in charge of their holdings while he "worked out." We liked him very much. He was from Texas, tall and rangy, and with a good knowledge of stock.

Mr. Laune had bought a herd of wild horses which he put out to pasture near town on Roundup Creek, and wanted someone, preferably Dan whom he could trust, to break them to harness and saddle before he offered them for sale.

Dan had a light, sure hand with the horses. He had a complete vocabulary too, that he used in talking to them in his pleasant, easy voice. Mr. Laune said he was gradually catching on to the language Dan spoke and would soon know it as well as the horses did. "But," he added, "better not let the children hear it too often."

Dan's ranch, which he had extended from a few quarters into a sizable spread, was northwest from Woodward more than forty miles. He was proud of the land and liked to talk about it, and about his wife and boy. They had the usual claim shanty, but Dan was ambitious to improve the place into a real working ranch. We never knew his wife, but he bragged that she was the smartest young woman in Oklahoma. And pretty? Man, you oughta see how pretty her hair curled, and her blue eyes shone!

"Isn't she afraid to stay alone so far from neighbors?" I asked him.

"Her? Afraid?" scoffed Dan. "Say, that girl can lick her weight in wildcats, if she has to. I gave her a gun and showed her how to shoot it. She can kill rabbits and quail, and once she killed a coyote. She could shoot any varmint she had to. Man, she sure can handle it. She ain't afraid of nothin'."

"But she, or the baby, might get sick. Something might happen to them and she couldn't let anyone know."

"Nothin's going to happen to them. We've got neighbors kinda clost. If anything did happen, she'd know what to do. That girl's smart, I tell you."

One night we had an early blizzard with an unexpected skim of snow. It grew freezing cold; a norther was blowing in the very best tradition. The wind, straight from the North Pole, blew cruelly sharp, like thin slivers of ice, cutting through and searching out all the thin spots in one's clothing, snatching away one's breath and making the throat and chest ache. The sun rode pale and high in the remote gray sky, and the wind—always the merciless wind—sent its frozen particles of sand against the face like splinters of glass. Dan went as usual to the pasture, where he worked the horses, and came in at night with reddened face and hands stiff with cold. He kept his eyes turned often to the northwest whence came the storm, and where lay his ranch watched over by the smartest girl in Oklahoma.

Next morning at the breakfast table, he said tentatively, "Boss, if you don't care, I'd like to mosey along home today. I've got—a, well, I've got some heifers there I'd like to see about. They're sorta breachy, and they might break out of the pasture in this storm and—wander. My wife she oughta not leave the boy when it's so cold, and he shouldn't be trailin' after her either."

We understood. Dan would not admit that his wife could not handle all usual situations alone, but the boy "sorta crippled her stride."

Wrapping his muffler around his hat which was pulled down over his ears, he bowed his head against the vicious wind and started off in the long swinging canter that we knew his horse could maintain for miles in ordinary circumstances. But this was not an ordinary storm and we saw him go with something like dread.

All day and night and all the next day the wind kept up its spiteful, stinging whine and the cold tore at the tightest, heaviest wrappings. Saturday night the storm died away, and Sunday, though as cold as Greenland, was beautifully clear and sunny.

Dan did not come back that day as we expected. Tuesday evening, just as we sat down to dinner, he strolled into the kitchen from the corral.

After he had twisted Sidney Benton's foot where he sat in his high chair, slapped Paul on the back and pulled Russell's curls, he grinned at each of us in turn and took his place at the table.

"How'd you find things at home, Dan?" Mr. Laune asked as he served the dinner.

"Fine, Boss."

"Find your wife and boy all right? What's the matter with your hand?"

Dan laughed. "Well, sir, you know, I had the darnedest, funniest accident. I told you, my wife, she can take care of herself. Well, she sure can. I don't needta hafta worry about her none." He looked at his bandaged hand and began to chuckle again. "The reason I didn't come back before today was account of this hand. My wife wanted to make sure it was all right."

"What did you do to your hand?" Mr. Laune asked again.

"Well, sir, I was plumb careless." He turned his hand over and looked at it carefully, and amusedly. "I shoulda known better."

"Tell us," prodded Mr. Laune.

Dan laid down his fork and settled back in his chair; we all settled down too. We knew we would hear a good story if Dan ever got around to telling it. But he could not be hurried.

"You know that—da—wind never let up all the way to my ranch?" he started out aggrievedly, looking around the table for sympathy. "Pete," he said, speaking of his horse, "and I just ducked our heads and hadta face all those miles. Forty-odd miles of that wind was sure some miles." He picked up his fork and began eating again. We ate too. After quite a while, he resumed. "It was kinda late when we got home. I hadta stop way up there near Supply to get warm. I was darned near froze." We all nodded again. "So I fed Pete, and had something to eat myself. Say, Mr. Laune, you know those folks. They're friends of yours. Mine, too."

Mr. Laune said, "About your hand, Dan?"

"Well, as I was saying, it was late when we got home. Musta

been halfway to morning. Everything was dark around the house, so I knew my wife and the boy were asleep. I was so near froze I could hardly stumble off my horse and stand up.

"I rattled on the door and yelled as well as I could; but my voice was froze, too. So I reckon, what with the wind ablowin' like—" he glanced around the table at the three children sitting there with their ears wide open, "—and bein' froze, like I said, my voice didn't sound right; 'cause when I hollered, my wife— she's darned smart, like I told you—hollered back in a kinda whisper, quiet-like, so's not to wake the kid, I reckon. She said, 'Who's there?'

"I yelled, 'It's Dan, let me in.' And I beat on the door again. But as I said, my voice was froze, and she said, 'Take your hand off that door.'

"She didn't say anything more for a minute, and I kicked the door. Darned near kicked a hole in the—well—thing; and near broke my toe. It was froze almost but hurt like—" he looked at the children again, and sighed.

"'Take—your—hand—off—that—door,' my wife said. 'Go to the shed and crawl in the hay. There are horse blankets and buggy robes in the shed, and you can keep warm there. You can't come in this house. I'll get breakfast for you as soon as it's light.'

"Well sir"—Dan was warming up to his story—"that was a pretty howdy-do. Here I had been gone more'n a month, and to be told to go to the hay shed. So I tried to break the door down, and hollered some—words. I was madder'n," he coughed. "When BANG! I thought the whole shanty had been shot to—" he sighed again, looked at Mr. Laune, and murmured, "you know where."

Dan turned his bandaged hand over and regarded it pensively. "You know what?" He grinned engagingly. "That darned little—ah—cutie, nearly shot my finger off. She sure did. I had it on the door latch."

Over the years we had acquired several farms, scattered through the county, and the problem of finding men to work

before as she leaned against her mother.

"Now, you see why I don't care for anything," the mother said bitterly.

I could see the angry red scar on the child's arm. It looked like a recent wound.

"What happened?" I whispered.

The woman raised her left hand and I saw that her fingers, except the little finger and the thumb, were gone.

"He blames me." She jerked her head in the direction of the room with the closed door. "Yeah, it's all my fault." She gave a short, bitter laugh. "I wish—" and her mouth curled in anger, "I wish to God we had froze to death. We nearly did."

The mother put the child out of her lap to the floor with a restless movement. The baby staggered to his sister and the two children sat on the floor to look at the pictures together.

I still could not speak. I felt sick in the pit of my stomach. She began to speak in a low, desperate monotone. "Yeah, it's all my fault. I took the kids and froze 'em." She gave again that short angry laugh, as she straightened in her chair. "Well, he drove me to it."

The door opened in time for the two men entering the room to hear the last sentence. "You heard me," she snarled at her husband while Mr. Laune stood still, the leases in his hand.

"Yes," replied the husband, "I heard you. I've heard the same thing dozens of times. And since you've started, finish it. Tell the whole story, but tell it straight. I'd sure like to know that the truth is told one time. All right, begin."

He stood, tall and stern, beating down her gaze with his steady, cold blue eyes. "All right," he repeated, "begin."

"Maybe you'd better tell it, if it's told," she retorted, starting to rise from her chair.

He pushed her back and stood over her. "Begin," he ordered, "I drove you to it. Go on from there. Tell how I drove you to it."

"Let's not quarrel before strangers," she said, in her sneering voice.

children on the floor. The mother rose and the children ran to her. The father picked up the baby, and they left the office.

But the arrangement didn't work out very well. After a time, the young man's surliness became hard for Mr. Laune to meet. The woman, so far as we knew, never spoke a civil word to her husband. A pall of hatred seemed to settle over the farm, and eventually Mr. Laune asked them to leave. But the memory of the maimed child and the bitter mother, maimed also, haunted me for years.

Some years after this when Mr. Laune had again been elected prosecuting attorney, a car belonging to one of our townsmen was stolen one night from where it was parked on Main Street. A short time after it was reported lost it was picked up at a filling station in a small town not far away.

The next morning the sheriff brought two young boys, about twelve and thirteen, into Mr. Laune's office. They admitted— they could do nothing else—having taken the car, but they were so frightened they could scarcely talk. That is, the younger of the boys was too frightened. The other one simply could not be coaxed to talk.

And again Mr. Laune called me over the telephone: "Put on your bonnet, honey, and come to the office, will you? I need you."

When I arrived, I was directed to the office of the county judge who was questioning the boys without getting any reply. The sheriff stood just inside the door and grinned as I entered, tipping his head in the direction of the two miserable children huddled on a bench.

"Big, bold, bad bandits," he muttered. "Poor little devils; they look like nice kids, too."

The blond head of the younger boy lay against the back of the bench; his eyes were closed and his breath came in gasping sobs that he tried pitifully to stifle. Tears rolled down his cheeks. His childish hands lay on the seat on either side of him, palms up.

The older boy sat with one foot tucked under him, regarding his companion with puckered brows, his brown eyes solemn with sympathy. He sat pinching together the torn rent in the blond boy's overalls, now and then patting his knee.

The judge, kind and understanding, leaned back in his chair and sighed as he nodded to Mr. Laune, who said, "All right, boys, stand up."

The brown-eyed boy stood. The blond head moved from side to side, the blue eyes opened in terror, as he attempted to struggle to his feet. His legs trembled so that I was afraid he would fall. Mr. Laune stepped beside him and braced him with a knee as the child clung to the judge's desk.

After the reading of the charge, and a short talk by the judge, the frightened boy gave a convulsive lurch toward a spittoon and was sick on the floor. The other boy watched with troubled eyes. Not a word had been spoken by either one, and we could not tell if they had heard and understood what had been said to them.

Mr. Laune drew me forward. "This is my wife, Mrs. Laune. We have sons; two of them. I think you can tell her the whole story, and she will understand."

We went in to Mr. Laune's office and sat down. Mr. Laune busied himself at his desk and I waited until the boys looked at me. It was not long before the brown-eyed boy began to talk, and then it was to complain of the blister on his rough hand.

"Let me see," I said.

Without a word of protest he put his hand in mine. It was red and swollen.

"How did it happen?" I said.

"We were working in the wheat field," he replied.

"Where?"

"I think it was in Texas."

The blond boy nodded, without speaking.

"Do you live in Texas?"

A guarded look flashed between them. They did not answer. We talked about Texas, and wheat, and cattle.

I rambled on about the ranches that I was familiar with. And then, before long, the story came out. They had run away from their homes in another state.

"But why?" I asked.

Cecil, the blond boy, told me that he had worked hard at home and was saving his money for the fall term of school. "To buy my books," he said, "and a school sweater. And I had enough to, but my dad took my money. He said he needed it; but he didn't ask me for it. He just took it."

Cautiously, we delved for the right address, and when we were sure we had it, Mr. Laune disappeared into his private office, and I heard him telephoning.

The boys were fairly launched by this time. They had a sympathetic listener and they poured their grievances out in a flood. Over and over, I would have to laugh and say, "Whoa, I'm all mixed up. Tell me that again, and try to talk one at a time so I can get straightened out."

Mr. Laune opened the door and motioned to me. When I rose, the sheriff appeared quite as though he had sprung out of the air, and took my seat, smiling lazily at the boys.

I almost laughed at the absurdity of guarding those two children.

Mr. Laune was talking again over the telephone, and using his most frigid voice. "The boy has stolen a car. He, and another boy. This is a pretty serious offense, and if what he tells is the truth, you should be the one to pay the penalty. The boy said that you took the money he had earned, and that he expected to use in going to school. When he found that he had no money for school, he ran away. Now he's in serious trouble. What are you going to do about it?"

He listened for a while. Then his voice altered. "I'll tell the boy." He turned to me: "Tell Cecil that his father wants to talk to him."

The boy's face turned scarlet when I told him. He looked at me as though I had betrayed him, and walked slowly into the inner room.

We listened to the one-sided conversation. After a long talk, the boy said, "All right, Dad; goodbye." And Mr. Laune took the telephone again while the boy and I returned to our seat. The sheriff evaporated.

"Mom's awful sick, Dad said. She's been sick ever since I left. He— he— said he was sorry he took my money, but he was going to pay it back. He said if Mom wasn't so sick, he'd—" a long pause, "he'd come—and" he gulped and couldn't go on until he got control of his voice, during which time the other boy, whose name I had learned was Jed, and I talked.

"Mrs. Laune, will they send us to the penitentiary for stealing that car? We just wanted to go to the oil fields, where we could get work. Pitching wheat was too heavy for us. But we thought we could get work in the oil fields. That isn't so heavy, is it? We wasn't going to keep the car. We just wanted to go to the oil fields."

Mr. Laune came back into the room. "Your father is sending your aunt here to be with you, Cecil," he said. Then he spoke to Jed. "All right, Jed, what about you? Do you want to tell us, so we can get to work on your problem?"

Jed shuffled nervously in his chair. "I don't know where my dad is. And I don't know where my mother is, either. They're divorced. My mother went away and I was staying with a cousin of hers. They weren't very nice to me, so I left."

"Do you know where any of your people are?" Mr. Laune asked.

"Well, I've got a granddaddy." The boy's face brightened. "I know where he is, I think. We went to see him once. Maybe he'd want me. You reckon you're going to put us in the pen? Or maybe the reform school?" Terror again flooded their faces.

It was not easy to locate the grandfather, but after several calls Mr. Laune was successful. He told where his son, the boy's father, could be found. He was in a hospital, with a broken leg. Mr. Laune hung up the receiver with a troubled air.

Jed was delighted that his father had been found. "But maybe, if he's hurt, he couldn't bother with me," he said. He began to talk about his mother, telling rather damaging things in a frank, open way.

"Is your mother an immoral woman?" asked Mr. Laune, after one statement.

The boy looked at him, perplexed. Then his smile flashed out. "Oh, no sir. She's pretty, and dresses awful nice. She's not im—what you said."

The next day Cecil's aunt arrived, a quiet, dignified woman, ready to do all that she could to help the boy. Jed looked very small and alone.

I don't know what legal proceedings were followed, but Cecil went home in the company of his aunt, and Jed was paroled to Mr. Laune. We took him home with us and I found some of Sidney Benton's clothes that fitted him fairly well. He was delighted with them; they made him look like a wanted child.

A week later, Mr. Laune took Jed to his grandfather, who really did seem to want him. He wrote regularly to us, telling us everything he was doing on the farm. "And I'm going to school," he added. "It's a nice school, and I'm on the team."

So there were some heartbreaking stories that had a happy ending, and others whose end we never learned. The wonderful thing about a small community like Woodward is that you know everybody—especially if you're a lawyer and the prosecuting attorney, or his wife! At least, it's wonderful if you like people, whether they are being sad or bad or funny or tragic.

14 You Can't Keep a Good Town Down

After the City Council had made two attempts to sell bonds for waterworks that were promptly frustrated, a movement was started way back about 1906 to grant a franchise in order to secure this much-needed commodity. The idea of a franchise did not please everyone but the needs of the town were desperate.

Mr. Sid Nixon, who hauled water in wagons from his springs, warned that during the coming dry weather the springs would not be sufficient to supply the growing town. So everybody began to worry about the slowness of the Council in providing waterworks and the newspaper became more sarcastic than usual.

At last, after more voting and more disappointment, a Denver company bought for five hundred dollars the springs and water rights of a farmer across the river and plans were made for a water system, soon to be followed by all sorts of conveniences: electric lights, cold-storage plants and goodness knows what else.

And the paper said there was no way to keep a good town down.

When work began on digging trenches for the water pipes we were all excited beyond telling. Every woman in town made —or at least dreamed of making—arrangements to put a bathroom in her house. When the diggers entered our block the children and I all but lived on the edge of the ditch, so that the workmen would say politely, "Stand back, if you please, Ma'am," over and over again.

But we couldn't stay away and we asked all kinds of foolish questions about the size of the pipes that were to be put in, and the depth of the trench, and so forth.

We were always answered patiently by, "Search me, Ma'am, we're hired to dig the ditches; we don't aim to know nothin' about the pipes."

At last the pipes were laid on top of the ground beside the open trenches, out of which I was kept busy pulling the children. After a long delay, the pipes were laid and covered, making wonderful-looking mounds all over the place.

But still there was no water.

Mr. Laune had pipes laid to the house, to the corral, and on each side of the house, to wet down the lawn and trees. And we waited. And waited.

Some two years later, when hope had all but died, muddy water that had traveled across the river was flushed from the mains—and a miracle like that which followed Moses' striking the rock, was enacted for the people of our town. Abundant, clear, sparkling spring water, without a taint of gypsum, poured into our homes. It was a day we shall never forget.

Meanwhile, to relieve the strain while waiting for the waterworks to be completed, Mr. Laune and a group of businessmen organized the Woodward Cotton Company. This company had for its prime motive the stimulation of cotton growing in the county, to be followed by the installation of a cotton gin.

Mr. Laune, who had never lived in a cotton-growing country, and knew nothing about its cultivation, was enthusiastic about growing cotton on all our own farms, and on all the other farms in the county. He anticipated beautiful fields of cotton blowing from the bolls; somebody would pick it, we would have it ginned in our gin, and then ship the bales somewhere. He was president of the company. He got together a lot of figures and statistics, and addressed the Chamber of Commerce. (Our Commercial Club became the Chamber Of Commerce, after we got water.) It was a splendid speech, the paper said, and they published it in full.

All the people who, like Mr. Laune, were ignorant of cotton raising were enthusiastic advocates of planting cotton. They donated money to buy seeds to be distributed to any farmers who wanted them.

There was, however, bitter opposition to the idea from those who had come from cotton states. They were loudly vocal in their declaration that they were not going to plant cotton; they had no notion of making cotton pickers of their children. And if the children didn't pick the cotton, they wanted to know, who in the world would?

Mr. Laune brought up that outworn question of a side crop that would bring in cash. Mr. Martinson repeated what he had said many times before, "Vell, I shust stick to castor beans. They do pretty vell for dis country, I t'ink." And the broomcorn growers said they would stick by broomcorn. It did pretty well, too.

If there was one thing that Mr. Laune thrived on, it was opposition. So, as soon as it was possible, we had beautiful cotton coming up on one of our farms. That fall it was white in the field, bursting the brown bolls, and waving in the breeze.

At the table one day, Mr. Laune turned to Mrs. Lafon, our good friend and neighbor who helped me with the housework.

"Mrs. Lafon," he asked, "did you ever pick cotton?"

"Why, yes, Mr. Laune, when I was a child in southeastern Oklahoma."

That was just what he wanted to hear. He beamed at her across the table. "How about your taking the field out at Woodlawn? Do you think you can get it picked?"

"Who would I get to pick it?" she asked intelligently.

"Can't your children pick it?" Mrs. Lafon had five children about the age of ours.

"No more than yours. They've never seen a field of cotton."

Mr. Laune looked at her as though she had said something clever.

"That's an idea," he smiled. "You and None take the children out on Saturday and let them pick the cotton."

"All right," she said, looking knowingly at me.

While we were washing the dishes we laughed about our children picking that field of cotton on Saturday. However, early Saturday morning we loaded the children, a lunch, and some grain sacks in the carriage and drove to the farm. Mrs. Lafon outlined the work to the children, gave them each a sack, and showed them how to get the cotton from the boll. Then she, and I who had never been in a cotton field, each took a sack and started picking.

At noon, we ate our lunch and the children thought it a most successful picnic. Then the smallest ones took a nap on their sacks.

At quitting time the cotton was weighed on the scales Mrs. Lafon had brought for that purpose, and an account was made of each child's picking. We went back several times after that, piling the cotton in a mound at the end of the field. At the rate the picking progressed, the children would be old, old people before the field was cleared. We never did finish it. After most of the cotton had been whipped from the bolls by the wind, and clung in dirty, grayish wisps to stalk and weeds, Mr. Laune made Paul "overseer" of a group of his young friends and they got out most of it.

However, the Woodward Cotton Company went doggedly ahead and built the cotton gin, and when it was finished a few men stood around a wagon beside it, on which were two bales of cotton, and had their pictures taken.

Mr. Martinson went on growing and buying castor beans and made money.

Nobody seemed to be very sorry about the failure of the cotton venture. The Woodward Cotton Company decided that Woodward needed electricity and it would be sensible to convert the Cotton Company into a light company and the gin into a power plant. So the new company bought a large Diesel engine.

The franchise was granted, the company advertised that it would wire homes and business houses, and before too long the town blazed with lights; you simply pushed a button or pulled a string! The most beautiful and comforting commandment ever given, "Let there be light," was demonstrated in a practical way. I had almost forgotten how wonderful it was to see a light bloom, like the silent, sudden opening of a flower.

But, again, the funds we had worked so hard to accumulate for the building of a new house had been depleted alarmingly by the Cotton Company. They were all but exhausted by the light company. Delighted as I was to have electricity I raised my voice in protest over the vanished money. We built another room. . . .

Later, with so much electrical power on hand, a flour mill was added to the company's activities, wheat being a major crop in the country.

There came a moment when I caught Mr. Laune drumming on the table with a look I knew; it meant he was dreaming up another scheme for the expansion of the town. I had had a hard day. I was not in a sweet mood when Mr. Laune murmured pensively, "I wonder . . . I wonder . . ."

I should have been satisfied, for Mrs. Lafon and I were washing with an electric machine—the first, I believe, in the town. However, soon after we pinned the clothes on the line, a gale began to blow. In no time flat, our lovely clean things were covered with black soot from the coal-burning railroad engines that labored up the grade south of the house. The wind snapped, pulled and strained at the long heavy line. The line broke. The clothes fell to the ground in the sand. They had to be washed all over again.

I murmured too, but not pensively, "I wonder, too, just when I can be relieved of *everything* connected with washing."

He smiled at me beamingly, snapped his fingers, patted me, said, "Good girl," and went to the telephone where he called one of the owners of the Electric Company.

"Can you meet me at the plant?" he asked. "I think I have an idea."

There was a small steam-laundry in the town in which we had an interest, but it was obsolete and unable to meet the town's increased requirements; it was bought and what we called an electric steam laundry was the outgrowth of the day's irritation.

This seems to be a good place to insert parenthetically that the modest funds we and other people put into promoting and building these various enterprises, never brought any of the investors a single kilowatt of light, a dusting of flour, or a garment washed, unless we paid the usual rates. In fact, this money never brought us anything except the supreme satisfaction we all felt in helping to "make the town grow."

Now that we were a City of The First Class, we needed another railroad, a road running north and south to open up the vast territory of wheat farms north of town. Soon we had that too.

The Launes built two more rooms on their house.

We were now going at such a rapid pace that we could no longer bear the uneven board sidewalks; we wanted proper walks.

Again we all stood up and howled for our favorite kind, or for the privilege of not having any at all. Some people wanted brick, and some concrete, and some just didn't want any. And the paper came forward as usual with: "There are some people in the town that do not want it to progress; they should sell their property and let someone who would join the forward movement of good citizens, have it."

We built sidewalks ten feet wide, made of concrete. The streets were graded and the little porch roofs or awnings that hung out from the front of the stores and shops were ordered removed. None of this was accomplished without loud and determined opposition.

When the long Main Street was graded, a young man who had succeeded his father in the drug business, refused to allow the removal of the old hitch-rack his father had had placed in front of the store when the town was in its infancy. Since automobiles had already largely replaced the wagons and buggies and teams that once lined Main Street, and since there was in any case a public wagon-yard, there was no longer any need for the hitch-rack and the city wanted it removed so that the street could be properly graded. All the City Council's persuasion and reasoning fell on deaf ears. His father had put that rack there, he repeated patiently. The posts were planted deep in the ground, and the boards that connected them were thick and stout. It was an honest piece of work, planned and supervised by his father, and it was going to stay.

"But," explained the exasperated Council and other businessmen, "it's no longer needed, and stands in the way of the new walks. We've got to get those racks out of the way."

"My father put those racks there, and they'll stay there," said the young man stubbornly.

The street commissioners worried. They wanted the matter settled peaceably, without the use of force or drastic measures. Nobody wanted any unpleasantness.

Then someone remembered an older brother who lived in a near-by city. He was called over the telephone and the matter explained to him. Yes, he understood. Of course the racks would have to go. He would see what he could do. In a few days, an invitation came from the older brother for the young man and his wife to come and visit them. The invitation was accepted, and in their absence the racks were removed.

When a new bank, the Central Exchange, was built, Mr. John Garvie, whose saloon closed when Oklahoma went "dry," was made president. In front of the bank grew a tree. Not a very large, and certainly not a beautiful tree. It was a scraggly, wind-worried tree, that was smooth of bark where horses had been tied and had rubbed against it for years on end. Mr. Garvie was attached to that tree; so far as anyone knew, it was the only thing in the world on which he expended any sentiment. It was not in the way of the walk, he contended, and no commissioner was going to cut it down. City ordinance or not, that tree would stand where it had stood during the years. They could build the sidewalk around it, or they could just not build a sidewalk in front of the bank at all as far as he was concerned.

Few people argued with Mr. Garvie. He had been a member of the Vigilantes in No Man's Land, where he had been a pretty important personage. No Man's Land was a strip of territory some one hundred fifty miles long and forty miles wide which somehow escaped the attention of any government, whether state, territory or federal. In the absence of any law, the settlers made their own agreements about property rights and organized the Vigilantes to control the activities of criminals and outlaws who, not unnaturally, considered it a happy hunting ground. When the strip known as the Cherokee Outlet was opened, No Man's Land became part of Oklahoma, and a picturesque episode in frontier history came to an end, though not before a good many dramatic and violent stories had been contributed to the saga of the West. Mr. Garvie was a quiet, courteous gentleman, but a determined character. If he said that tree was not to be disturbed, all of Woodward, almost, would have bet that it wouldn't.

But if the town was going to have a sidewalk ten feet wide, and a tree stood in the way, what could you do? The commissioners wanted to know, and stood on the corners, and asked all and sundry. The work on the sidewalk was held up.

People took sides for and against the tree. Many who had never noticed the tree before became its champion. "It don't take but a few days to lay a sidewalk, but by gum, it takes years to grow a tree, and we ain't got too many of 'em." They grew sentimental. "It ain't like Uncle Jack had a wife and children; all he's got is that tree; whyn't they just let it be until he dies." Mr. Garvie at that time looked as tough as a cedar in the canyon, and as if he might live forever.

By this time the City Council had its back up, and decided to make an Example of the tree. "Why looky here," they argued unhappily, because they liked Mr. Garvie and really hated to cut down his tree, "if we let every tree and hitch-rack and horse-trough along the street stand in the way while we fight about them, we'll never make any progress."

Mr. Garvie took the matter to court; but the judge shook his head sorrowfully. The city was right. The tree was cut down.

It was also ordained that only brick buildings could be built on Main Street, and for one block on either side of the cross streets. The streets were named for the first time and the country roads were also improved.

Each advancement, I repeat, was accompanied by loud cries of anguish from those who opposed it. But once the decision was made, everyone worked for its success. Peace, or a reasonable facsimile thereof, descended, while loins were girded for the next battle.

15 Business Interests: Various

The men of the town were continually alert to find new activities which might benefit the community and the surrounding countryside and, as the climate had proven to be peculiarly adapted to poultry raising, they decided to organize a Poultry and Pet Stock Association, with Mr. Laune as president. It was a wonderful idea, for more money can be made sitting around the table raising poultry and selling eggs than any other way I know.

Everyone concerned was to raise a different breed; I remember that Mr. Jim Herod, who owned the dry goods store, chose Barred Rocks, and Mr. Hoag, our county treasurer, chose Buff Orpingtons. Mr. Laune chose White Wyandottes, and paid more for them than we could afford. Before they got through, I'm sure every variety of chickens, turkeys, ducks, geese, and pigeons were among the selections made by the members of the Poultry and Pet Association.

Mr. Laune bought his first chickens just before the exhibition which was to be held in the town. He had little idea as to what was required of a prize-winner, and was as excited as a mother with her first baby at a baby-show. On the other hand, the person from whom he bought the chickens certainly must have known a great deal about poultry for Mr. Laune won all the prizes given for White Wyandottes. After our fair was over, the chickens were sent to other fairs where they won more prizes.

We subscribed for a poultry journal and, in his enthusiasm, Mr. Laune sent to Canada to a firm that advertised in it. He paid a lot of money for a setting of eggs, from which one solitary chick was hatched, and that chick, he told me sadly, was a "sport." The next year, he ordered a cockerel for some sinful sum, and the drayman delivered the bird at the house when none of us were at home. He set the crate with the new rooster in the yard, and our old rooster, who must have resented the beauty of the newcomer, promptly pecked its eyes out. There was deep mourning in the House of Laune.

We learned that showing chickens, where there is strong competition, is a highly specialized work. We also learned that vanity was not lacking in our feathered friends.

The chickens were bathed and polished and beautified before each show. They accepted the handling quietly, and it seemed that they tried to assist in the work; our old rooster certainly knew much more about the procedure than we did. After having been bathed (as they were white chickens it was permissible to put a little bluing in the rinse water) they would stand on their boxes before the oil stoves, preening and turning, lifting their wings, and raking their bills along their feathers until they were dry and glistening. They sang contentedly while their legs, claws, beaks and combs were manicured, and submitted gracefully to the oiling and polishing. They seemed to know that if they fluttered and strained to escape their handlers, their feathers would be mussed and mutilated, and they would be disqualified.

Just before one of the fairs in which Mr. Laune was going to show his birds, he drove them into the chicken house and found that the big rooster, which he was sure would take the prize over all birds of all breeds shown, had wallowed in some tar that had been emptied in the yard after a roof had been repaired.

He was distracted. Taking the big fellow in his arms he went to the wash house, where Mrs. Lafon was struggling with Sidney Benton's white blouses that were also liberally touched with tar.

"How can we get this tar off this cock, Mrs. Lafon?" he asked her.

"Search me," she responded cheerfully. "The only way I know would be to cut the feathers off."

"You can't do that!" Mr. Laune replied horrified. "That would disqualify him, and ruin my reputation."

"I'm using gasoline to get it out of Sidney's clothes," she said. "Does it work?"

"Just fine."

"Do you suppose it would work on this chicken?"

"I don't know. It might." She rubbed away, and Mr. Laune saw the tar come out.

"Come on," he suggested. "We're going to wash this fellow in gasoline."

Mrs. Lafon demurred. "I'm terribly busy, Mr. Laune; I haven't time to wash that chicken. Anyway, gasoline might not take tar out of feathers, and it might kill him."

He and Mrs. Lafon had shared many trials together, and were a good working team.

"We'll try it anyway," he said.

She wiped her hands and they got a tub of gasoline ready in which to douse the bird. Sure enough, the tar began to come out. They scrubbed and laughed happily. The whole matter was solved slick as soap, and the bird was clean.

But when they put him on the floor, he couldn't stand up. With a silly, weak "cawk," he toppled over on his head.

"Oh, my land sakes! We've killed him," cried Mrs. Lafon.

"Go call None," he told her grimly. "I think we have."

Mrs. Lafon came running into the house calling me to come. When I entered the wash house, Mr. Laune was watching sadly, while his prize bird went tumbling and lurching across the floor, giving out occasional pitiful cries. With his head ploughing the floor, his legs and wings flopping weakly, he made valiant efforts to get to his feet.

"We've killed him," mourned Mr. Laune. "He's dying."

I picked him up in my arms and carried him outside into the fresh air. I blew in his face and ruffled his feathers, fanning him with my apron. I thought the glazed look was leaving his eyes, but he still seemed sick. I petted him and fanned him some more, and he closed his eyes, every little while trying his voice in a tentative weak cry. Mrs. Lafon prepared a bath of clear fresh water and we washed the gasoline from him, petting and comforting him. Again I sat outside with him bundled in my apron, until at last, he seemed stronger and struggled to be free.

He went to the fair and won all the prizes in his class, and I have a noble silver loving cup inscribed with his record.

Another time, the entire flock went on a debauch. Mama and I had made jelly and jam from plums and peaches. We threw the seeds and peelings into the chicken yard, where they fermented in the hot sun. The chickens ate the stuff and became silly drunk. They had a hilarious party. They squawked, flopped and lunged weakly into each other, ploughed their limber heads into the ground, and tried to stiffen their dragging wings. Finally, they gave up and lay in grotesque abandon all over the yard, with closed eyes.

It was the best argument for prohibition one could devise.

Our post office was so inadequately housed in an old building (Mr. Laune's office was upstairs) that the people of the town grew ashamed of it. Most of the old buildings on Main Street had already been replaced by brick buildings when the report from the Postmaster General's Office that one hundred thousand dollars business had been done the year before in our post office made us think that a more imposing office should be provided through which all this money could pass.

Mr. Ben Key, Mr. Laune, Mr. Cline and Mr. Anderson, and perhaps some other businessmen on the west side, formed a joint stock company for the erection of a building. As is the way of our town, violent opposition rose to placing the post office on the corner of Tenth and Main where this company wanted it, and the merits of other locations were loudly argued.

When the inspectors came to pass on the location, it was suggested by Mr. Key and Mr. Cline that it would be an act of courtesy for Mr. Laune to take the inspectors quail-hunting. Our county was famous for quail, and it seemed only kind to let the visiting inspectors enjoy some sport. Of course, there could have been no idea of keeping the visitors away from those people who had other plans for the location of the new post office.

Mr. Laune started out with Dixie and Yankee hitched to the buggy, and enough ammunition to defend a garrison. They drove across the river into Hastings' pasture. Mr. Hastings had given cheerful consent. He was a member of the stock company and had property near the site of the proposed new building.

It was the opening of the quail season, and the birds flew in extravagant numbers from the natural hideaways. The strangers had never seen anything like it.

The team was left standing in the tall grass while the men scouted through the brush. Mr. Laune never hunted with dogs. With a rushing whirr, the coveys were flushed, and the bombardment was on.

All of a sudden there was a frightened, wild neigh from Dixie. She and Yankee plunged through the brush and high weeds, the buggy bouncing behind them. Mr. Laune shouted, but, strangely, they paid no attention. Around and around the pasture they flew. There seemed little Mr. Laune could do but let them run until they tired themselves out.

When at last, breathing heavily, they stopped in the corner of the barbed-wire fence, he found Dixie's rump covered with blood. She had received a full load of bird-shot. He was pretty cross, and whispered in her twitching ear what he thought about the carelessness of hunters. He was afraid that she might be gun-shy after this experience, but evidently Dixie understood that only "city fellers" were ignorant and careless with guns.

The inspectors approved the building site and the plans for the building, and on its completion the post office moved into the lower floor, while Mr. Laune and Mr. Cline each had a suite of offices above.

For a time after that, life moved along smoothly. No project was currently distracting Mr. Laune. Mama and I went to the clubs and church societies; the children were in school; Fan was working downtown; and as we sat together in the evening, Mr. Laune read aloud to us while Mama, Fan and I sewed or cro-cheted and the children studied.

Then a man came to town with equipment for making concrete blocks for building purposes. He worked in a lot down by the railroad tracks. Mr. Laune watched as the man tamped the wet cement into a mold, and after carefully removing the mold, left the blocks in the sun to dry. He was, as always, greatly inter-ested in watching a process new to him. Finally, he asked if he could tamp awhile. The man released the implement with a nice show of reluctance, and stood by giving instructions that Mr. Laune tried his conscientious best to follow. You must use so much cement, so much sand, and so much water; these you mix thoroughly, shovel the mixture into the mold, and tamp.

As he hated to be having all this fun alone, Mr. Laune took me down to the lot and asked the man if he would permit me to tamp a little while. Consent was graciously given. Then they both stood by and gave me instructions in making cement blocks. It didn't seem very complicated, and I hadn't had so much fun since my mud-pie days.

The law office was in danger of being deserted as Mr. Laune could not stay away from that cluttered old back lot.

"Why None, it's wonderful," my husband told me, gravely. "It's the best building product in the world; especially in our country where we have neither timber nor stones."

He bought books on the subject, and sent to Washington for more information. Now, while Mama and I sewed, he read to us technical articles on concrete, instead of enlightening us with the history of Napoleon, Disraeli, and howling over The Mistakes of Moses, by Ingersoll. E. P. Burdick used to go with Mr. Laune to the lot, and hunker down beside him, and together they would watch the blocks pile up. They decided to get into the business, have some fun, and maybe derive some revenue from it.

About that time, a young man came to town from the country near where Mr. Burdick had a farm. He had recently lost his young wife, and was the most desolate person one could imagine. He wanted work, and Mr. Burdick said that here was the very thing—the cement-block business. So Mr. Burdick and Mr. Laune bought out the business, lock stock and barrel, moving the entire outfit up to our place north of the house; the blocks could dry under the long sheds where the broomcorn had been stored. Also, it made a more convenient place where Mr. Laune and Mr. Burdick could sit and watch.

Clarence was introduced to the forms, the sand, cement, and water. Day after day, week after week, he doggedly pounded out his grief, trying to develop a philosophy that would help him face the future. By this time Mr. Burdick and Mr. Laune had invested in quite a library that Clarence studied during every spare minute. With sublime confidence in Clarence's ability as an engineer, they backed his competitive bids on quite large, pretentious enterprises, such as a livery stable which perhaps will remain to demonstrate the indestructibility of concrete.

The absence of bridges and culverts across the unpredictable streams in the county had always been a handicap, but many had argued that it was a waste of money to bridge a stream that was dry for most of the year. However, during the rise of water the farmers across the river were cut off from town for days at a time. That was not productive for anyone. And now that automobiles were coming into general use, bridges were needed across the sandy draws. Something had to be done. Clarence consulted with Mr. Burdick and Mr. Laune about building these culverts and small bridges. They thought it was a fine idea if he could manage it. So he secured contracts for those he thought he could construct, which were so successful that he became more and more ambitious, and wanted to bid on the bridge that was badly needed across the wide North Canadian River.

At this time, I believe, the company consisted of Mr. Laune, Clarence, and me, Mr. and Mrs. Burdick having gone away on one of their frequent long trips. We three went into a huddle and decided to make the plunge. Mr. Innis, who had been our county surveyor for years, made a favorable report on the location, Clarence secured the bid, and the material was hauled out. Men were obtained to help and Clarence went to work.

The bridge was to be an imposing structure across the river about nine miles east of town, near where the Santa Fe had a railroad bridge. Everything was going splendidly, we thought, until one morning about three o'clock there was a pounding on our front door. I hurried into a robe and opened the door. There stood Clarence, in a terrible state.

The piles that he had specified in his contract were found to be much, much too short. After having been driven down into what he believed was a solid clay bed, they suddenly entered a deep layer of quicksand. Piling of more than half again the length he had thought necessary, as well as other changes in material, would have to be used to make a solid bridge.

"That will not only take all the profit out of the contract, but load you with a big debt," he explained miserably. "I can't tell just what the loss will be, but it'll be big."

After a long moment, Mr. Laune said, "You contracted to build a bridge that would stand through high water, didn't you?"

you can interest her in meeting some of the members of our chapter."

"Why, of course," I responded, and went to be introduced to the visiting stranger.

I think she was the saddest person I had ever seen. There was such hopelessness, such a withdrawal from all contact, that she did not seem to be in this world at all. I found myself inclined to shout at her as if she were deaf, but she could hear perfectly.

I tried to bring her into some sort of conversation. I asked, because I did not know how else to approach her, innumerable questions that I hoped would sound like sympathetic interest rather than curiosity. And at last she did begin to talk in a hushed, monotonous voice.

When I asked her where she lived, she replied with the name of the county where oil had recently been discovered in rich quantities.

"Oh, do you live near that oil field?" I asked.

"That well"—the one the papers were lyrical about—"is on our farm."

"Why, how wonderful!" I exclaimed, looking at her with renewed interest.

"No. It's not wonderful," she replied in her faraway voice. "It came too late."

"Oh, did your husband die before the well came in?" I asked, not knowing what to say, and thinking how dreadful it would be to have such a miracle happen, and not have the dearest person in the world with whom to share it.

"He died after the well came in, but it wouldn't have made any difference. It came too late."

I knew from the papers that she must be receiving a fabulous sum for her share of the wealth that was pouring out of her ground. I could see her poor, gnarled, work-worn hands folded in her silk-covered lap, and tried to find a comforting word. "Well," I floundered, "it's a comfort to know that you won't have any financial worries. It is dreadful to be alone; but . . ."

"No. That ain't no comfort. I'd rather have it the way it was.

They ain't nothing to do!" She sat and stared into space, hope-lessly.

"Maybe you could have fun building a new house." To me, that seemed to be the pinnacle of bliss.

"What for?" she countered.

The picture of my four, my family, rose before me. "What for," certainly, if you could not share the joy with those you love.

"I never had a silk dress before," she twitched the silk with distaste, "and it ain't even comf'table. I wisht, oh how I wisht, things was like they was before." The cry came from a tortured soul.

"Yes," I agreed softly, "but we can't go back, and your children will enjoy what the oil will bring."

She turned her haunted eyes to me. "How kin they? They worked in the coal mines and the cotton fields from the time they could work. They ain't got no education, 'cause they never went to school, much. My children was worked to death when they was young, and all their lives. Now, they say they ain't goin' to work no more, ever. I can't blame them. Now, they just lay around spending money for things they don't want, and don't know what to do with."

"Well, it will be fun to give your grandchildren an education. You'll enjoy watching them learn and grow," I said, brightly.

"No," she refused to be encouraged, "it's too late for them, too. They don't cherish no hunger to learn from books. The money is ruinin' them too. I wisht it was like it was.

"We lived in a dugout when they was little, and then we built a little house. The children worked hard, but they useta laugh and have jokes. Now they quarrel about the money. They quar-rel fiercest about the way to spend the money. They made me build a big fine house, and I'm lonesome in it. The folks that built it put in a lot of things: pictures on the walls; books in the bookcases, and I can't read them very well. Not enjoying the reading, I mean. They put dishes in the cupboards, and there are a lot of them that I don't know what to do with. And a lot of silver in a shiny box; and I don't know what all the funny forks are for.

"I wisht I was back in the little house that didn't have no carpets on the floor. But it's tore down. My children are fighting and don't speak to each other. And my grandchildren are purt-nigh ruint with the money. They buy whisky and carry on. We useta never have no money; and now, we don't know what to do with it. It come too late."

The gavel called the meeting to order, and I was glad to stop trying to talk. Throughout the meeting the poor woman sat with her hands twisting the despised silk dress, bought with the money that came too late.

On the whole, we had a lot of fun with our business enterprises; even if they interfered with a new house, we felt they were, one way or another, important. Of course, there were a few hundred other people who thought, as we sometimes did, that *they* were dragging up the town singlehanded and alone, without any sympathy or cooperation from anyone at all. We couldn't understand the stupidity—Mr. Laune called it bullheadedness—of those whose policies differed from ours. Why in the name of common sense, didn't they fall in line with our plans instead of making it so hard for everybody (us) and retarding the progress of the town?

But somehow, when the opposition went right ahead, while we pulled as hard as ever we could in the other direction, and things still turned out all right—or at least, the town didn't fall apart in one big crash—we cheerfully admitted that the foundation on which it rested—which *we* of course had built—was pretty solid.

16 Events Foreseen and Unforeseen

Mr. Len Stine, who was the president of the First National Bank, our third bank, had the first car, I believe, in town. It was a White Steamer, almost as large as a Santa Fe locomotive, and required an engineer's license to operate it.

The first time Dixie and Yankee saw this juggernaut come snorting and leaping down the road, they stopped, stunned, in wild-eyed fright. It must have seemed to them sheer folly to try to combat such a monster and for a moment they stood trembling, then dropped flat and buried their faces in the sand.

Then a number of people bought cars. Mr. Laune could not stand seeing so much pomp and circumstance around without having a part in it, so he "dickered" with a man and came into possession of a Ford touring car. He drove it to the house, parked it at the carriage block, and went in search of me. Fan and Russell discovered it and in his absence they got in and drove away.

When I went to admire the new possession there was nothing to admire. We looked all up and down the street, but no car was to be seen. Then we discovered that we had no girls.

"Russell took that car," said her father, heavily. "In a little while we'll get word that she's wrecked the car and killed herself and Fan. Can't you teach her anything?" he asked me.

After what seemed like a long time, during which we had all gone into mourning, we heard the car. It came rolling up to the curb and stopped, bucking only slightly. Fan and Russell stepped out. Russell took her father's arm and pointed to a deep dent in the brass band around the radiator.

"You see," she said chattily, "I didn't know how to stop it. We were doing nicely, but down that little hill into Spring Creek, there was an enormous hayrack piled full of hay. I couldn't stop the car, and I couldn't make the man driving the hay hear me, so I slammed into the back of his wagon. It's a shame the car got bent, isn't it?" She viewed the mashed radiator sadly. Then she began to laugh. "Fan and I were nearly buried in the hay that toppled on us." She sobered. "The man started to scold me for spilling his hay, but I told him I didn't know how to stop the car, so he showed me."

Her father swallowed a few times, sighed wearily, shook his head and walked back into the house.

Some time later when we had a new Studebaker, I was entertaining callers on the front porch when Russell and her friend, Katharine Brewer, came strolling up the street to the house. I didn't notice them getting into the car.

Suddenly we were almost deafened by the screaming of the whistle, and the tootle-te-toot of the switch engine on the track a block northeast of the house. We looked up, annoyed at so much noise, and someone remarked that a car was stalled on the track over the grade. That was none of my business; the engineer and fireman were pushing the car across the track and the engine was puffing behind them. At that point, I noticed that our car was gone, and Russell and Katharine were nowhere in sight. Then I saw our car going merrily down the street about two blocks east of us.

With a prayer of relief, I started to pay attention again to what was being said by my visitors, when again we were assailed by the same frantic tootle-te-toot. Russell, now a block south, had stalled the car on *that* crossing, just in time to stop the long string of boxcars again.

I was just starting to fly down the road to her rescue when I saw the men again doing their best to push her over the tracks. In a few minutes the girls came onto the porch and greeted the guests. Russell explained that the gearshift was different from the other car. Seeing me limp and shaken, she said:

"Why Mama! Were you frightened? Don't you know those men wouldn't run over me?"

My own experiences in driving were not very happy. I much preferred Dixie and Yankee and the carriage to the car, and when I was in the car I preferred to have Mr. Laune, or one of the boys, drive. The boys learned to drive by instinct when they were entirely too young, and were good drivers. When I was with them alone, they would explain: "Now, this is the first thing you do, then this, and this. Do you understand?"

I would try to look intelligent, nod my head brightly, and agree that I understood. And this mendacity was almost my undoing.

Mr. Laune expected any member of his family to do anything that needed to be done at the time of need, never mind if there had been no preliminary training. You just automatically knew how to do a thing if the necessity arose. That was the way he reacted, and he honestly thought everyone else did the same.

We had a farm about twenty miles west of town where we

loved to go for summer camp, and where Mr. Laune kept horses, mules and cattle on the excellent pastures.

One day at noon, he said, "Put your bonnet on. I have to take some horses to Fargo to the pasture, and I want you to drive the car. We'll take the equipment for the camp today, too."

I looked at him in astonishment. "What did you say? You want *me* to drive to Fargo? Don't be ridiculous; you know I can't drive even as far as the office."

Mama looked worried. She almost never questioned Mr. Laune's wisdom.

"Do you think Nonie can drive to Fargo, alone? You know, she isn't a very—experienced driver," she said.

My entire experience had been to drive through the gate at the pasture after Mr. Laune had gotten out to open it. But he was always near enough to jump into the car and take charge.

"Oh yes," he answered Mama, easily, "she'll do all right."

I still thought he was crazy and would come to his senses in a minute, but he began loading the car. There was a small wood-and-coal-burning stove and the pipes for it, barrels, tubs, pots, pans, cots, and bedding, with everything else necessary for the camp. All this was piled and tied inside and around the sides of the car. The top of the car had been folded back to make room for more stuff. He always moved like chained lightning and was soon ready.

"Here." He tipped up my chin and tied my sunbonnet under one ear. "Hurry," he shoved me into the car. "All set?"

"But I can't do this, you know," I protested.

"Sure you can." By this time he had pushed me under the wheel. "Now, show me what you do to start."

"You do this, and this, and this." I waved my hands above the gears without touching them.

"All right," he nodded, leaning across the door, "now do it."

"But I can't stop it," I cried.

"Well, don't stop it; I don't want you to stop it until you get to the pasture gate, then turn the switch off and wait until I get there. It may take quite a while, because I shall have to go

slowly. I have to lead these two colts. All right, get going."

With shaking hands, I did this, and this, and this. I could hardly believe it—the car left the curb! Mama watched me with despair written all over her face.

"I can't turn around very well," I shouted back.

"All right, don't turn around," floated to me above the rattle and bang and din of equipment. "Just keep going."

About two miles from town runs Spring Creek, the same creek where Russell jammed the Ford into the hayrack. There was no bridge, just a built-up ford across the shallow water.

As I was heading down the long, low hill into the creek to cross the narrow ford, I saw a car approaching me, coming swiftly down the slope on the other side. I knew I couldn't stop my car, and I knew that I was going to slam into that other car.

The wind was blowing a gale, and my sunbonnet was flapping across my eyes. The pots and pans, buckets and stove and all the other things dangling and bumping and rattling and bouncing all around me, made the din of a riveting machine sound like a sweet echo.

I leaned forward over the steering wheel and began to yell: "Get out of my way. Can't you see that I can't stop this thing? I'm going to kill you!"

The driver of the other car couldn't hear me above the wind. He didn't know his danger, and I hated to do what looked inevitable to me. I'd just better kill myself, alone.

I let go the wheel and grasped the brake with both hands, shut my eyes and pulled on that stiff stubborn brake lever. The car wasn't going more than eight miles an hour maybe, but we smashed against the bank on the other side of the creek with a jerk that almost jarred my teeth out, while stars spun around my head. A voice shouted at me angrily, as the man leaned over my car door:

"What in the devil are you doing out on the road with a car? And how did you get in such a condition in a bone-dry state?" His eyes grew wide with amazement. "Good Lord! It's Mrs. Laune."

By all the canons of fact and fiction, I should have fainted.

That was what I wanted to do—just quietly and completely pass out. Then he would have to take me home.

But instead of doing anything so appealingly reasonable, I burst out crying and smeared sand over my tear-drenched face, and explained that Mr. Laune thought I could drive to Fargo, "and I ca-a-an't."

While he was patting my arm, and sympathizing with me, Mr. Laune rode up with the colts cavorting around him. He tied the horses to the fence and the man spoke to him sternly about letting me attempt to drive twenty miles in that car when it was evident that I should not be allowed to go twenty feet.

Mr. Laune's lips thinned out in the well-known, will-you-attend-to-your-own-business line. He thanked the man politely for his interest and turned to me.

"You're doing beautifully," he assured me quietly. "You've come nearly two miles. If you can drive two miles, you can drive twenty. You don't have to think about driving to Fargo, just think about driving one hundred feet ahead of you; then, another hundred feet. You're doing beautifully." He tinkered with the brake and other things, pulled the car back into the road and up the little hill, and said:

"You're all right? Now go ahead. If you get tired, turn out of the road, turn off the switch and wait for me to catch up with you. I'll be coming behind you as fast as I can."

Somehow, I don't know how, I did reach the pasture gate. I promptly slumped down in the seat (after turning off the switch) and went to sleep. After that drive I expected to see every hair in my head as white as cotton, and deep wrinkles of age in my face, but I didn't seem to be much changed.

People in town learned of the trip and teased me about it. And because I always drove slowly and carefully on our streets, one day our marshal, seeing me coming, made a megaphone of a newspaper and shouted: "Clear the street! Clear the street! Here comes Mrs. S. B. Laune racing down Main Street at six miles an hour."

We lived a mile from school and there were the railroad tracks to cross, as I have mentioned. The boys were seldom late, but Russell's report card showed an embarrassing number of tardy marks. When her teacher questioned her, she explained brightly, with her engaging smile:

"You see, I have to cross the tracks and there is nearly always a train on the crossing. I c-o-uld crawl under," she would pause for a horrified refusal of anything so dangerous, "but my mother has told us never to do that."

If the teachers had ever thought to mention that Paul and Sidney also crossed the same tracks, I don't know how she would have answered. The matter didn't disturb her at all, but I could hardly hold up my head when the list was published in the paper.

None of them would carry a lunch and they weren't willing to eat lunch downtown. They preferred, even on the coldest, most blustery days, to face the wind coming home and be blown back to school. Their father would wait at the foot of the stairs as the children passed the office on their way home, and in a few minutes we would hear the four of them laughing and running and puffing. They always raced each other from the tracks.

Perhaps the coming of a hungry family home to meals is the happiest memory a mother has; at the time, there is always so much bustle and confusion, that she doesn't know how much it means.

Russell had been taking piano lessons since she was eight. I explained when she began that I was much too busy to "make" her practice, and she realized the truth of that. She promised she would do her practicing without compulsion. But I found it a good plan to say, as we rose from the dinner table, "You run along and practice while Mama and I wash the dishes." As long as she heard the rattle of dishes in the kitchen, she practiced diligently. I devised a scheme of putting some cutlery in a pan, and while I sat beside the cabinet and read I would shake the pan every little while. I don't know whether she ever suspected my ruse or not. She learned quickly and it became a family custom for Russell to play hymns, popular songs, or old favorite melodies while her father and the boys stood behind her and sang, almost every evening.

One night, as Mama and I were sewing, and singing along with the rest, I looked up and saw my family. Really saw them with every sense alert. Russell at the piano; her father behind her with a hand on each of her shoulders; a son on either side of him, an arm linked through his; all of them singing lustily.

I saw them so plainly that I was startled almost into a chill. Something seemed to say, "There is your beloved family, your world, look at them! Never forget that picture. The time will come, when you will not have it so."

I dropped my sewing on the floor, stumbled to my feet, and went to stand behind my husband. I slipped my cold hands in his pockets, and burrowed my forehead between his shoulders.

He took his hands from Russell and put them in his pockets over mine. Turning to me in surprise he whispered, "Are you ill?" I shook my head, and the boys sang on. "What happened? Your hands are as cold as ice."

"Nothing. Really, nothing at all." I was shaking, and he led me to the couch where we sat down together.

"Something must have happened to disturb you."

I shook my head again, and tried to smile. After we had gone to our room and the lights were out, I tried to tell him of the sudden feeling of coming desolation. Of loss.

"It was a kind of premonition, a presentiment, a—a—hunch," I shivered.

"By golly, if you can't conjure up the darnedest things to scare you into a green chill. You are absolutely the biggest idiot I ever heard of," he laughed, shaking me gently to break the spell of fear. "Of course there will be changes. We all change from day to day. The pictures change. Of course they do. The youngsters will grow up, go away to school, get married, go into business. We've lost the picture of tonight already. It's gone, and another will take its place. Now go to sleep."

But I could not forget it and go to sleep, and for days fear haunted me, until the children looked at me queerly, and asked, " 'Smatter Mom? You feel all right?"

I never did forget it. It would pounce upon me when they were all talking at once, and laughing around the table, and I would turn sick and cold as I did that night when they were at the piano.

It always seemed to me—though I am exaggerating a little—that nothing was ever quite the same after the sinking of the *Titanic*. In our town, so far from the scene of disaster, I wept for Alfred Rowe, who would never again return to his Texas ranch; and for all those others who went down in that icy sea. Hard on that tragedy, a series of terrible floods filled us with sympathetic anxiety. And in 1914, the papers screamed that an Austrian archduke and his wife had been assassinated by Serbian conspirators in a town with an almost unpronounceable name. Europe had seemed as far away as the heavenly planets, but from that time on Mr. Laune read the papers to Mama and me every night.

However, it had really very little to do with us, we thought, and we were certainly happy in our Oklahoma home. After a while we became again preoccupied with the usual parties and club meetings and civic upheavals. Russell and Paul were in high school and their friends and parties kept them happily busy. Sidney Benton was in grade school, and the PTA, which was new then, was important in my life.

When Russell was graduated from high school, we planned to send her to a girl's school in Nashville, Tennessee. The Mississippi River with its unpredictable vagaries chose to go on a rampage, and Mr. Laune took a stand.

"No," he said, "I shall not put that river between us and our only girl. Surely, there must be a school on this side, that can teach her something."

While we were debating, a representative from a school in Missouri came to town to solicit pupils, and called on us. We knew a number of girls who had attended this school, and were persuaded to send Russell there.

During my conversation with the representative, she remarked that she had just come from Amarillo, Texas. I had been in Amarillo a number of times, and I said that I thought Amarillo was a lovely city.

She looked at me incredulously. "Lovely?" she repeated. "What's lovely about it?"

"Why—why—" I stammered. After all, how can one describe the beauty of our western plains? There is not a tree, a hill, a stream, not a thing that is known as "scenic beauty."

"It's lovely," I repeated, feebly. "You can see so far."

"What can you see?" she asked, reasonably.

I gazed at her, as puzzled as she was at me. We simply did not see the same thing. I saw the city rising firmly and solidly from the plains in a vast pasture where cattle used to graze, built without benefit of native tree or stone, beneath skies of incredible blue through which one's gaze goes up and up in the pure clear air until it seems that the very gates of Heaven are revealed.

The clouds of such whiteness that drift across the blue sky; the colors that meet and blend with the prairies, so pure and clean and delicate. If she had not seen all this, I could not describe it to her. I could only repeat, that it is the most beautiful country in the world. But I could not put this beauty into words. There is something so honest and forthright in its very simplicity. It does not need hills and streams and forests. There is the sky and the earth, all the prismatic colors shifting and blending, with nothing between. The sun comes up in the morning in a sudden radiance. No coy peeping in and out, retiring behind hills and trees. No shilly-shallying. There it is, in full splendor. And so, in the evening, in the full power of its light, the sun goes burgeoning behind the horizon. And darkness falls.

Several times after that, I tried to make other-minded people see the beauty of our West, once when we were in Wyoming visiting some friends. Now I think Wyoming is beautiful and grand, but I cannot feel the comforting assurance in a mountainous country that I do in my own plains and prairies. Mountains disturb me. They are too encompassing. I feel cabined, cribbed, confined.

This man in Wyoming was telling me how beautiful were the mountains. "And," he said, sweeping his arm in a circle that took in the towering peaks rising bare, bleak and cold on every side, "nowhere in all the world are there such sunrises and sunsets."

I thought of my prairies, with the flaming sky turning to pink, blue, purple, mauve, and amber. "Oh, no," I replied quickly, "the morning and evening skies of Oklahoma and Texas. They are more lovely, more dramatic, and besides, more gentle—" I hushed. I saw he did not agree with me. This was his home, his sky, his mountains.

And then, there was a woman in Washington State. We were driving from Seattle to Bremerton, and on into Canada to Vancouver, through marching ranks of hemlocks, spruce and pines, standing straight and tall and remote, like the dim aisles of a vast cathedral. And she was saying:

"No place in all the world are there such lovely trees, so splendid and majestic; I love the spruce more than any other tree, don't you?"

And I thought of the wind-worried, cattle-rubbed elms and cottonwoods on our dry prairies. Of the long crooked branches where swings can hang, and little children sway dreamily back and forth. Of their leaves that turn and whisper and gossip in friendly intimacy. I have not been in all the world, so I can't talk about all the trees in far distant places, but I could not imagine leaning against one of the stiff, dignified spruce in that hushed dim forest. They were not for me, prairie-lover, and loving our trees in that prairie land.

And I knew a tree in Oklahoma, where I have driven with my husband many miles to sit and eat a lunch beneath its haven of shade; where a hundred cattle can bed and sleep beneath its protecting branches. One tree, magnificent in its splendid size and majesty, growing alone in that wide friendly space. I still can hear my husband say:

"If I had the money to spend as I like, I would buy this tree and protect it from prairie fires, so that the cattle might continue to browse and drowse beneath the shade of its branches. This is the most beautiful thing I know."

But to return to Russell. She went to the Missouri school that fall, and we missed her cruelly. We missed her ever-ready laugh, that started bubbling like a fountain released, rising to a shower of merriment and ending on a half sob, like that of a baby who has laughed too long. We missed her jokes and teasing, and the piano. We missed the invariable question that came every morning when she poked her head out of her bedroom door and called: "Mama, what dress shall I put on?"

We pounced on her letters, so funny with their schoolgirl phrases and comments. We were disturbed when she wrote that she was slowly starving to death, and drew a picture of herself as a famine victim. Her father was so worried over the fact that his only daughter did not have enough to eat in "that darned school" where *I* had sent her, that he could not enjoy his own meals.

"Can't you send her some nourishing food?" he asked me, fretfully.

So I sent her a basket of food that I thought would be nourishing, and hoped it would sustain her for a while. She wrote and thanked me gratefully.

We decided that if she were too emaciated when she came home for Christmas vacation, we would not send her back. After all, there was no profit in sending one's beloved daughter away to starve.

When we met her at the train a day or two before Christmas, we couldn't believe our eyes. The faded flower that we had all but met with an ambulance, bounded off the train so fat that her cheeks were like round pink balloons. Her eyes shone, and her hair fairly crackled with well-being.

"But they feed us things that make us fat, and leave us hungry," she explained. "We can't go to the refrigerator whenever we want to, and I want fried chicken and hot biscuits every day while I am at home." Evidently she was not concerned about a sylph-like figure.

"Do you want to go back?" we asked.

She looked astonished. "Why, of course I do!"

Driven deep within me, hidden and forgotten most of the time even from myself, lay the terrors that had accompanied the growing up of our three. These terrors would sometimes haunt my dreams and waken me to a cold, trembling chill. From these troubled dreams I would turn to the secure bulwark of my husband. From his broad back and deep rhythmic breathing, I would draw comfort and reassurance.

If, in our waking hours, he suspected that I was obsessed by fear he would laugh. "They've grown up, haven't they? All whole, intelligent, and good-looking. Where, oh where, is your faith?"

But I could not forget the time when I saw Russell's lips grow purple and heard her cry with a sudden clutching at her breast, and learned for the first time of her fall from a tight-rope she was trying to walk.

I thought of the time she ran the needle through her finger when she and Angela were sewing on Mrs. Abbott's machine. She ran across the street to her father who took her to Doctor Rose where it was dressed. When I rebuked her for her carelessness, a neighbor child looked at me accusingly and said: "Her papa kissed it, instead of scolding her." Thereafter, "her papa kissed it," became an overworked phrase in the family. I thought of the time she stuck her finger in the bone-grinder to hasten the grinding of the bone meal for the chickens, and nearly lost it.

And of the time Paul had "walking typhoid." And of his operation for mastoid, when I rushed with him to the hospital in Kansas City where Evelyn and Joe Williams held my hand through three dreadful days of doubt.

And of Sidney Benton, when he drank nearly a whole bottle of Mama's sweet-tasting cough syrup containing chloroform. Of the frantic hours we spent on each side of him, holding a limp little hand as we dragged him, heavy with sleep, up and down the block, and bathed his face with cold water, and shook him to keep him from going into such a sound sleep that he might not awaken.

And of the times all three had been thrown from their ponies and, later, the boys from bucking bronchos, scaring me into a green panic.

But here they were, in spite of all these happenings and dozens of other frightening incidents that occur in a family of active, adventurous children. Russell and Paul were beginning to talk of marriage, Sidney Benton was growing up fast, and owned a motorcycle which I considered a fiendish invention, all noise and smell and speed. It bucked Sidney Benton into a barbed-wire fence, a long way from home, cutting his leg seriously; I hated it, but one day downtown the horrid thing whizzed past me, with Mama sitting in the sidecar, her white hair blowing and a smile of perfect satisfaction on her face!

No one should have been surprised when our country went into the war in 1917. I suppose we weren't, in a way, but the shock of the reality had not been cushioned by all the warnings.

Certainly, our town did not take the war calmly. Our people worked day and night, making speeches, pajamas, and robes, hospital gowns and dressings, snipping rags for stuffing pillows, with everybody supervising everything. We saw our boys off on the trains, and met trains, carrying boys from other towns, with baskets of sandwiches, cookies, and cigarettes—the latter things of evil that we had made laws to suppress. And, I must admit, running around getting into each other's way and making lots of noise. Businessmen made speeches about patriotism, standing on the floor of a truck where everyone could see and hear them: "Fellow-citizens, we shall shed our last drop of blood—" It made me sick when I saw whose last drop of blood was to be shed. Certainly not the blood of the man standing on the truck, or any of us older ones, immune from the demands of government, handing out cheer by the basketful. I could not stand it. I could not bear to watch those smiling boys hanging on to the rails of the observation cars, waving to us until there was nothing to see except the tracks stretching out for miles and a little speck that was the train.

One day, the president of our newest bank asked me to come to his office to talk over a "matter of importance." He was a most attractive, persuasive young man. He told me that he, as chairman, had suggested me for his assistant chairman to the Liberty Loan Committee in our district of eight counties.

I have the most un-executive mind in the whole world. I can't add two and two and be sure that four will inevitably result. I had spent a good deal of time in my life trying to keep people from finding out about my deficiencies, so while I was pleased that I had succeeded in fooling such a nice young man, I knew that if I accepted this responsibility he wouldn't be fooled long. I smiled, and thanked him for the compliment he had paid me, and firmly declined. Then he made a speech on patriotism that surpassed anything I had heard and I walked out of the bank the duly-appointed and acting—whatever my title was.

Almost before I had finished telling Mr. Laune what I had agreed to do, I was called into Oklahoma City by the state chairman, Dr. Andrews, for a meeting with all the other vice-chairmen of the State Liberty Loan Committee. And to top it off, I developed an attack of ptomaine poisoning from something I had eaten when we stopped in the dawn's early light for breakfast.

The state chairman was a practicing physician. She sat at the head of a long luncheon table, where we were to discuss many weighty matters dealing with the war and the Liberty Loan. She watched me curiously as I sat quietly dying, then she came swiftly to my side, got me out of the room, called the hotel drugstore, gave me something, and put me to bed. I missed the whole meeting. It was just as well. I couldn't understand what all those smart women were saying, anyway.

When I returned home, white and shaky, I was sure of only one thing. Anyone who knew as little as I did needed a lot of competent women to act as sub, or county chairmen, to assist her. I promptly got busy and appointed them.

There followed weeks of pure bewilderment, and the hardest work I had ever done. I rarely left my desk after that except to go on what was called "speaking tours" over the district. Every day I received reports from the eight counties giving the number of bonds that had been sold. Long columns of figures that had to be added! By me! I almost wore out my ten fingers and ten toes. I had Mr. Laune check the results because I was so impressed with the necessity for having them correct.

All the counties met their quotas. The telephone and telegraph bills were so large they worried me. The bill to one of the county chairmen who lived a long distance away, and could be reached only by messenger boy from the telephone office, was enormous. I was ashamed to send it to headquarters for fear it would cause a national scandal, so I just let Mr. Laune pay it.

Meanwhile Russell had become engaged to Ed Hopkins, who was a cadet at West Point; Paul was studying art in Chicago and burning with impatience to play an active part in the war—a state of mind his parents unpatriotically (he thought) failed to share. He and a dark-eyed schoolmate had made all their plans to marry when "it was all over." Sidney Benton, like other boys his age, was restless and annoyed at being too young to enter the armed forces, though to his father and me the margin of safety seemed very narrow. If the horror would only stop! We were among the lucky ones, and we knew it, and very often felt almost ashamed in the face of other people's tragedies.

When the end of the war came at last, I remembered an old colored woman we used to know. When she got up in the morning to a beautiful day, or if anything pleased her especially, she would say to Mama: "Lawdy, Miss Sally, I'se feelin' so good I don't want to tell lies about my neighbors."

That is the way we felt after the Armistice, for a little while at least; we felt so good we didn't want to tell lies about our neighbors.

But of course, we didn't maintain that exalted feeling of gratitude, contentment and good will very long. It might not have been good for us if we had.

17 So to the End

With the war over, we had time to look around and notice how many changes had taken place while we had been too busy to think about them.

The town had grown beyond belief. New people had come in and occasionally assumed control of some of our enterprises. Sometimes they even stood up in the Chamber of Commerce, the churches, and the school-board meetings and told us what to do and how to do it. That took courage, and somehow proved them worthy of living in our town. For perhaps there is no tighter circle, no greater aristocracy in a Western town than that of the pioneers, or First Settlers. They are the dictators.

The women's clubs had such a definite system of procedure that they had not changed much. We went on studying the classics in literature, the great masters in painting, with a paper on Modern Trends in Home Furnishings, or we sandwiched in something that would lead to better civic conditions.

The card clubs, however, turned from euchre and whist to auction bridge. I presume, in a way that might be considered progress. And if there is one thing we brag about in our town it is that we are progressive.

One day Mr. Laune told us that there was to be a demonstration of the "radio" at our Convention Hall, and he wanted Mama and me to go with him to hear it. We had read about the wonders of this "radio," but had never seen or heard one.

There was quite a crowd gathered when we entered the auditorium. A young man and his assistant bustled back and forth and round about a small black box placed upon a table. Electric wires were strung here and there. The man who was in charge fiddled with this and that, and made a little talk, and looked important, while we all sat silent and expectant. Then the lights were turned off except on the stage where a small light sputtered and glowed. There was a slight buzzing noise, but finally it stopped.

We sat and waited and whispered in the darkness. "What will happen if it works?" I asked Mr. Laune.

"We'll hear a voice from somewhere—Wichita, I believe," he whispered back.

The buzzing began again and the lights on the stage blinked. Nothing else happened. We sat there a long time while the two men fussed with the apparatus. It grew late. People began to tiptoe heavily out, but I knew we would sit there until morning, or as long as the men moved about the table on the stage. Mr. Laune was not one to desert a sinking ship.

After a long, long time, the lights in the hall came on and the man stepped to the front of the stage and announced: "Ladies and Gentlemen, the demonstration that we have been trying to bring you cannot be completed owing to——" and there followed a lot of strange terms that I did not understand. So we too went home.

After a few weeks, we went back for another trial. This time there were a lot of squeals and squawks and sputterings. But no voice from Wichita, or anywhere else. A third time we went again and really did hear a distinguishable voice. We could not get over the wonder of it.

Then our friends began buying radios and we were invited to hear them squeal and squawk and make a terrible racket. Each time this happened they told us it was because of "atmospheric conditions," and "static," and such things. They said that, usually, they got "perfect reception" and had no "interference" whatever. We got pretty discouraged.

Once when we had gone to a spiritual seance the table refused to tip, and the "voice" refused to "come in," and we were told that it was because we were not "sympathetic." So we began to feel uncomfortable when we were looked at suspiciously and told that the unresponsive radio was acting in a "most unusual manner" and "I can't understand what can be the matter; last night we had perfect connections with Duluth, or Chicago, or Kamchatka. . . ."

So we learned to decline invitations to come over and hear the radio perform. We made up our minds that we didn't want a radio of our own. Our family caused enough confusion without that.

It was all black magic to me—and still is—but I wonder how we ever got along without it. I would just as soon try to get along without my back teeth. Of course, I suppose I could nibble along with my front ones, but I would miss a lot of fun.

In 1926, we had a bumper wheat crop. The whole country was one vast wheat field. As far as the eye could reach, there were fields of waving green. Everybody had a good crop.

The sun shone from the blue, cloudless sky. Farmers talked excitedly. Combines worked night and day. We sat in the car and watched the wheat, heavy and yellow, swept from the field, the grain pouring into the bin, or hopper, while the straw was scattered over the land.

The elevators could not hold all the wheat that poured in from the fields. Mountains of wheat were piled on the ground by the railroad tracks. There seemed to be an almost continuous mound on both sides of the tracks of the new railroad that led to the northwest and into the Texas fields.

It was a joyful day, for we had had a long series of bad years. (Mr. Laune used to say we could expect a good crop only once every five years.) Because of lack of feed, the stockmen had lost heavily on their cattle, and the banks which had been trying to "carry" farmers and stockmen, began to fail. The Gerlach Bank—the bank that had begun business in a tent the day the town was started—was the first to go. The New State took over the building, and perhaps the few assets, a little while after. Then the Central Exchange and soon afterwards the New State and the First National closed their doors.

There seemed to be as many parties and entertainments as before, but we did not have as elaborate menus. They were just as good, because each hostess outdid herself to prepare attractive lunches with the least outlay of money. Tables were set with the usual glittering array of crystal, cut glass, silver, Haviland china and damask, but we did not send away, as formerly, for any luxuries. We did without, used substitutes, or invented clever dishes ourselves.

One woman on a farm, who found that she could not afford to buy sugar for her family, supplied them sweets by making a syrup of the juice which she pressed out, boiled and strained, from watermelons.

"It isn't very good," she said simply, with no embarrassment, "but it costs nothing, and it's a change. It answers until we have a wheat crop."

I never heard of anyone applying to the county for aid, unless there was prolonged illness in the family, though they may have done so. The people had accepted the restrictions brought by bank failures and dry weather, without losing their sure belief that money would eventually come again and happy times with it. If wealth was delayed for a time, no great matter.

Now, with so much money coming in from a good wheat crop and from the cattle that were feeding on green pastures again, the City Council thought it a good time to pave our Main Street. If certain requirements were met, the state highway department would give a helping hand.

But as usual, we had a period of some months during which we all argued for and against.

Our Main Street was a long sandy swath that cut through the prairie and extended for twenty-two blocks through the town. Most of the time it was a sandy, dusty lane, bordered on both sides by stores and shops, down which the wind scuttled, picking up every loose thing and whirling it merrily through the air. The town had bought a street sprinkler which was operated by the businessmen who paid for having the street in front of their places of business kept damp and dustless. Of course, there were dry patches now and then, where certain businessmen refused to pay. All day, every day, except during those rare times when the rains fell, the sprinkler plied up and down the sandy stretch.

Some citizens wanted a brick paving, and others wanted concrete. Some didn't want the paving to be a part of the highway, and others wanted the highway extended through the town. A good time was had by all, as usual. But finally, it was settled, and work began on a concrete paving the length of Main Street. Bonds had been issued, and taxes were increased.

I suspect these arguing sessions were good for the town. At least, every side of the question was aired, and no one was ignorant of the question under advisement—though, like me, they might have been befuddled. No one had a chance to "put anything over." Everybody had his and her say.

When the paving was completed, everyone was so excited about it that we drove up and down the twenty-two blocks of smooth concrete, and then started all over again. In our enthusiasm, we decided the side streets must be paved also.

That done, we felt we were really a metropolis. Surely no city could boast of more conveniences and luxuries. Surely there was nothing more for us to work and argue and fight for. We could sit back and indulge in a long life of smug contentment.

That was what I thought; Mr. Laune felt differently. He had never relinquished his old dream of conserving storm waters, of a dam at the junction of Wolf and Beaver Creeks, of a small dam on each farm, of "a lake on every farm."

Old Man River continued to go on wild orgies every now and then, flooding the valleys and bringing ruin and destruction to numberless people, besides dumping the topsoil from the farms into the Mississippi River, and finally into the Gulf.

Standing in the lush, rich fields of bottom lands in these valleys of the Mississippi, the Ohio, and lesser river basins, looking up the grassy slopes of the levees, which were the only protection from the rivers that rolled high above the land between the banks, he would become almost frantic at what he considered the stupid plan of the engineers who advocated this system.

"There are two schools of water engineers," he wrote in countless letters to men in Washington and those influential elsewhere, and in articles for the papers, in which he begged people to wake up to the necessity for a better method of control. "First, the conservationists, who believe in impounding the storm waters in great reservoirs, for irrigation, for reclaiming arid lands, for protection of the people, cities, and farm lands from torrential floods, for climatic changes, and for the pleasure of the Isaac Waltons.

"Second, there are those, who in seeking safety from floods, devise ways and means for running the water out of the country between levees and spillways. . . ."

He attended the Flood Control Conference in Chicago following the overflow of 1927, as a delegate from Oklahoma. There, he renewed his acquaintance and friendship with many men whom he had met at previous conferences and conventions for the purpose of discovering methods to control and conserve the storm waters.

When he came home, he was discouraged because the same old plan was evidently going to be followed. More and more levees and spillways.

He wrote, "When Congress convenes, one of the major problems for consideration will be flood control of the Mississippi River and its tributaries. In view of the disastrous floods of 1927, and the failure of the levee system, the government will be asked to make a very careful survey of the whole drainage territory to determine a plan by which future destructive floods may be prevented. Not for one year or fifty years, but for all the coming years."

We ate and slept with the question ever before us, and ever unsolved. I wished that he would forget the whole matter, and let the government worry along in their foolish way with the plans they evidently intended to follow. But he could not rest. The articles continued to be written and published. There were others who felt as he did, and editors were willing to give space to his ideas. It seemed to be a losing battle, yet he never admitted the possibility of defeat. That had never been his way, as no one knew better than I.

In the spring of 1928, as soon as the weather would permit, Mr. Laune began to plant a large apple orchard on our farm. Every morning, at the crack of dawn, he would jump into his "fatigue clothes," rush to the farm, and superintend the planting of ten thousand Stark Golden Delicious apple trees that he told me would make us rich in our old age. I didn't believe a word of it, and fussed at the hard work he was doing. His idea of "superintending" was to take the pick or shovel or whatever, and dig or pick, himself. He loved it.

From the farm, he would hurry home, take a bath, dress, eat his breakfast, and go to the courtroom. When he closed the office, he hurried home and, again in fatigue clothes, would go to the farm and work until dark drove him home. I lost my breath protesting that he was working too hard, and under too great pressure, but he laughed it off.

One Sunday morning, he said, "Let's go to the section in Texas today. Let's play hookey and not go to church."

It was sixty-five miles to our place there. It was planted in wheat and we had not seen it since the fall day soon after the wheat was sowed. Now, a little past the middle of March, it would be green and high in the field.

The day was perfect. I was glad to have him out and away where he could forget the depressing cases that were worrying him, cases connected with bank failures, and involving men whom he liked, but who he thought were guilty of criminal care-lessness, if not actually deliberate wrongdoing.

We turned west to the Texas land that we both loved, just over the border. The sloping prairies were turning green, that first tender green that is a promise of rich pastures for cattle.

The rabbits darted over the land and stopped to rest beneath the sagebrush, their bright eyes glittering. Meadow larks rose with a trill of song and settled on the swaying wire of a pasture fence. Mourning doves called, and the scissor-tails flaunted their long spreading tails. A gentle wind was stirring the young leaves on the trees we passed.

"Oh beautiful, beautiful land." He grinned at me, because I had accused him of saying this sentimental line so often.

We began to sing hymns, and old songs that he and Russell had always sung together—"Smiles" and "A Long, Long Trail."

He patted my knee and began a poem by Kipling that he never failed to recite whenever we started on a long trip. I had thought that he might forget it this time, and was glad he remembered. His gray eyes shone as he turned to me and began,

"The Lord knows what we may find, dear lass,
    And the Deuce knows what we may do. . . ."

No one was at home at our place; probably everybody had gone to church.

The wheat was beautiful. I sat in the car while Mr. Laune walked through it. A sea of green as far as I could see! On every side, from horizon to horizon, was green wheat, with the blue sky binding it all around the edges.

"Oh beautiful, for spacious skies, for amber waves of grain," we sang, as we drove up the section line on to Follette, a small town on the railroad spur. There we had dinner at the hotel; a dinner fit for kings—fried chicken, hot biscuit, mashed potatoes and gravy, asparagus, and canned green vegetables.

There were men in the hotel lobby who had heard Mr. Laune speak and had read his articles on flood control. They gathered around him. "We're going to dam a draw on my place, save the water, and make a lake." "Wish you'd come to my place, Mr. Laune, and look at the irrigation project I'm putting in. I threw up just a little dam in a hurry, and by gum, it's made a lake big enough to make good irrigation for my garden."

We drove home by starlight, after a perfect day.

But the next morning he said, "I've got a darned pain somewhere." He beat his chest.

"Where? Where is it?" He never complained and I was instantly alarmed. "Show me where."

He chuckled and moved my hand over his chest. "You're a blessed idiot. Do you want to pull it out with adhesive tape?"

Years and years ago, Sidney Benton had fallen in a mess of sandburs and covered his little hands with the tiny stickers that I could not get out with a needle. I smeared glue over the surface and spread gauze over it. After the gauze dried, I stripped it off, taking the little burs with it. It was quite a scheme, and saved a lot of pain.

"Will you go to the doctor and find out about that pain?" I coaxed. "Or will you go to the farm and plant a few hundred trees?" I finished sarcastically.

"Yes, I'll see the doctor, when I have time," he answered indifferently. "I'm all right."

Court that week was one long nightmare. Not only were the bank cases up, with lawyers from Enid and Oklahoma City opposing him, but some boys in the town got into trouble, boys whom we knew and whose parents came in desperation to ask his advice and help.

He came home at noon one day and did a very unusual thing. He lay down on the couch.

"Are you ill?" I asked him. "Is it that pain?"

"Just weary," he said.

My heart turned to ice. "Something's wrong. What is it?"

"Nothing serious, yet. Just boys going through a thoughtless phase that could lead to more serious consequences. They aren't bad. But I don't know how we're going to stop them."

"We can't. You sound like a—a—philosopher, trying to save our young people. Did you see the doctor?"

He rose and laughed. "I sound like—who was it? Plato, who wrote that young people were going to the dogs, or something like that? That isn't philosophy. That's just plain foolishness—senility. Yes, he said it was indigestion and gave me some calomel."

I hit the ceiling. "Calomel!" I shrieked. "Calomel went out of style with the dodo. Nobody takes calomel anymore. It's dangerous."

This was on Friday. That morning I had been awakened by something cold and damp pricking my cheek on the pillow. A tiny bunch of the first flowers of spring; wild pink crocus and dandelions, their heads pinched off without any stems, as he always gathered flowers. I put them in a saucer of water on the breakfast table.

There was to be a dinner at our church that evening. I had a part on the program, and the library board, of which I was a member, was to meet at the library building across the street from the church, just before dinner.

When he took me to the board meeting, he said, as he got out of the car, "Do I have to go to that dinner? Can't you just let me go home and come for you after the party is over? It's been a hard day in court, and I'd like to go to bed."

"Of course," I replied. "You go home and tell Mama. She'll give you your dinner, and you go to bed. Don't bother to come for me. Somebody will bring me home."

I went home early. Because he was not with me, the party was not much fun. I went into the bedroom and told him about it, making it more amusing than I had found it. He laughed so loud that Mama called out, "Come and tell Fan and me, if it's that funny."

We did not sleep because of "that darned pain" that kept nagging him. We lay and talked. About a trip we were going to take to New York to see Paul and Mary his wife and our little grand-daughter, Sidney. "Pretty wonderful youngsters, aren't they, bucking New York, and finding a place for themselves there." And we talked about Russell, who had spent two years in the Philippines with her Army husband; the tropics had not been kind to our girl, and we were thankful when they came home, bringing their baby, Nancy Ellen. "Russell hasn't a fault, has she?"

"Oh, plenty of them," I replied, laughing.

"All right, you name one," he said, contentedly. "I'm glad Ed's going to be stationed at Fort Sill. It will be wonderful to have them near us.

"And look at Sidney Benton in New Mexico. He likes his work, and the men like him. I'd like to send him to engineering school this fall. I'm glad he's going to marry Grace. He'll settle down and do some good studying, I believe. Pretty nice children you have, Mrs. Laune. And another grandchild coming. I'm glad."

And later he said, "It won't be long now before they have the gas laid in Woodward. How do you think you'll manage, not having to bother with coal or kerosene?"

At four o'clock I called the doctor to give him a pill. "And bring your stethoscope. I believe he must have taken cold. He has to get some sleep before he goes to the courtroom, Doctor, or he'll be dead on his feet."

The doctor laughed at my worry. "His lungs are as clear as a bell. There's nothing the matter. He's been working too hard, and has some nervous indigestion. Go back to bed and stop worrying."

I told him about the calomel that some doctor who happened to be in the office had given him. He threw back his head and laughed when I said I thought calomel had gone out of style.

"Go to bed." He patted my arm as we stood together at the front door. "There's nothing to worry about," he repeated. "If he doesn't go to sleep, give him another pill in an hour."

We couldn't sleep, even after the second pill. At six o'clock, he gave a little whimper of pain, and was gone.

He could not hear me call to him.

I flew to the telephone and screamed, "Send me a doctor!"

"Which doctor?" asked the operator.

"Every doctor in town," I answered, and rushed back to the bed.

"Come back!" I called to him.

For the first time in so many years, he did not hold out his arms to comfort me when I needed him. Not an hour before, he had asked with a teasing smile, "What would you do without your daddy?" And I answered comfortably, "I couldn't do. No one has to do what he can't do."

How many times that foolish question had been asked and answered in the same light way!

People came. First Mama and Fan. Then everyone in town. The doctors said it was angina pectoris. I asked what that meant and they said, "Heart."

Someone told me the boys would be coming soon, and later Russell would be with me. Our children, of whom he was so proud.

I only wanted to be alone with him.

"Do as she asks," Mama said quietly, and they all left me—the kind people, people I had never known but who knew and loved him, people from my church ("Mr. Laune's church" I had called it) and my own friends, people with whom I had been happy, whose sorrows I had shared. . . .

I sat with his hand in mine and said the things to him I wished I had said before. I listened, straining every nerve, trying to hear his answer.

Color, the lovely herald of the sun that comes with burgeoning banners, flooded the land, and he was not there to see it. He, who always rose before the sun. No pinched blossoms this morning beside my cheek.

A mourning dove began its complaining cry, ending with three sobbing notes, and then the answer came from its mate, comforting and near, the tender "there, there, there," like a gentle pat or a loving rebuke.

Even then, in my darkest moment, I knew that my husband, like the mourning dove's mate, would never be really far from me, that something of him would always be near to comfort me.

And so it has proved to be.